IF IT WASN'T LOVE

Bernárd Lynch has been at the forefront of theological debate and political activism since the 1980s. His candid and provocative account of his life as a gay priest will fascinate readers gay and straight, of all faiths and of none.
Michael Arditti, Author of seven highly acclaimed novels, most recently *Jubilate*

A companion book to Bernárd Lynch; *A Priest on Trial*, *If it Wasn't Love* shines a necessary if often uncomfortable bright light on the personal, political and spiritual dimensions of our half-understood and half-lived sexuality.
Jim Cotter, (Cairns Publications), ordained Anglican, author of *Good Fruits, Pleasure, Pain and Passion*, and *Quiverful*.

Bernárd Lynch is a gay Catholic priest with a husband, a fact that will draw some readers in and put others off. But those who delve in his book from either end of the spectrum will be surprised, challenged and gratified by his compelling and harrowing story and liberating message of freedom through love. There are rewards on every page.
Andy Humm, co-host and co-producer, "Gay USA" TV programme

This is a personal story inscribed in pain and passion, discovery and breakthrough, with a transparency to truth that feels as shocking as it is liberating. Would that we had more people who could be so incarnationally honest and real.
Diarmuid O'Murchu, Missionary, Author, and Psychologist

The moving personal odyssey of a brave, idealistic gay Catholic priest, from hope to despair and back to hope again. An inspiring testament of how truth, love and compassion triumphed over lies, hate and indifference. Bravo!

Peter Tatchell, renowned Human Rights Activist

It is reported that angels, forlornly searching the earth for signs of life in the wake of the human and ecclesiastical devastation caused by AIDS and the responses of Church officialdom, spotted Bernárd Lynch half submerged in the rubble. Stunned at the rarity of what they were seeing, they beamed back to HQ: "By God, a human! A living human being!". May these pages give you, as they gave me, a sense of wonderment at the holy possibilities of the stretched human heart, and the broad, broad priestly shoulders, which Bernárd is bearing up from under the weight of intolerable loss.

James Alison, Priest, Theologian and Author

A personal and powerfully engaging account of a priest's struggle as a gay man in the Catholic church, to remain true to himself and his faith in the face of the authority of the church and extreme persecution. He brings to his experience a depth of understanding and analysis.

Sylvia Hutchinson, Group Analyst

Bernárd Lynch was a pioneer in NYC in his work with the GLBT Catholic community and he was one of the first to institute a ministry to AIDS victims. We sorely miss him!

John McNeill, Priest and Author of classic work *The Church and the Homosexual*

If it Wasn't Love

A Journal about Sex, Death
and God

If it Wasn't Love

A Journal about Sex, Death
and God

Bernárd J. Lynch

Circle Books

Winchester, UK
Washington, USA

First published by Circle Books, 2012
Circle Books is an imprint of John Hunt Publishing Ltd., Laurel House, Station Approach,
Alresford, Hants, SO24 9JH, UK
office1@o-books.net
www.o-books.com

For distributor details and how to order please visit the 'Ordering' section on our website.

Text copyright: Bernárd J. Lynch 2011

ISBN: 978 1 84694 918 0

A CIP catalogue record for this book is available from the British Library.

Design: Stuart Davies

Printed and bound by CPI Group (UK) Ltd, Croydon, CR0 4YY
Printed in the USA by Edwards Brothers Malloy

We operate a distinctive and ethical publishing philosophy in all
areas of our business, from our global network of authors to
production and worldwide distribution.

CONTENTS

DEDICATION
for
My husband, Billy M. Desmond

Acknowledgements

My Readers:

Father James Alison
Michael Arditti
Father Jim Cotter
Andy Humm
Bryan Bernard Lynch
Michael Mulligan and his husband, Laurence Yang
Jane Robson
Laurence J.F.Wrenne

An Explanatory Note on the Layout of the Book

The Journal Entries can be read separately from the narrative/Seasons. Some of the journal entries may require a second reading, as they were originally written, as separate pieces for different audiences, of different disciplines. The 'Seasons' maybe read consecutively as they are autobiographical and follow in chronological order.

Preface

"Some people see things as they are and say why? I dream
things that never were and say why not?"
(George Bernard Shaw)

This is a book about life, love, sexuality, death, and God. It is
many people's stories, but most of all it is my story. Some of it has
appeared in other books, articles, and magazines, some in
homilies, talks, and lectures given on three continents: Africa,
North America, and Europe. These are stories birthed by fear
and oppression and redeemed by love. It may not be an easy
book to read, but I believe it is worth reading. For me it has been
both a challenge and a testament to my search for meaning in
what is often described as a meaningless world.

When I first started putting it together, I had some scattered
ideas as to how I would do this. With the help of my talented and
skilful editor, and the advice of some friends, the 'movie' in my
mind became more crystallised and clear. Some of the 'scenes,'
written in the early 1970s and '80s were never intended to form
part of a whole. They stood alone, as a lecture here or an article
there. It is my hope and belief that the book/story/'movie' holds
together as one man's attempt to be honest with God as I understand Him or Her. I hasten to add that this is not your standard
religious book. The words erection and resurrection, masturbation and Holy Mass are all found with equal authenticity, pain,
and celebration. It is no book for the pious or those seeking a
quick fix. The 'god of the gaps 'is not found here, or if he is, it is
as no panacea for our eternal thirst for meaning.

In this book, I owe so much to so many people who have
formed my mind, influenced my thoughts, and honed my
attitudes. Apart from my formal education, there are the
hundreds of books, articles, and papers I have read, digested,

regurgitated, and made my own. They are now part of me, and I would like to thank all of those anonymous mentors without whom I would have been the poorer. As Meister Eckhart would say, "All prayer can be summed up in the prayer, Thank you."

Introduction

Sexuality and spirituality ultimately become one. From being split and divided at birth, they are seen as the one source of the same river that flows through all of our lives. The truth becomes one, and truth makes us free even though it may crucify us in the process. I believe that freedom, not happiness, is the precious stone of life.

To have the freedom to imagine an interior world without fear is the first giant step in our quest to be human. To be born is to be human, but it is also to become human. Becoming what you have it in yourself to be is the mark of personal existentialist meaning. In fear there is no love or freedom. In love there is no fear or slavery. The opposite of love is not hate, but fear. Fear leads to hate as our world so well testifies. This apotheosis of fear transformed into love is the freedom hewn out of the rock of truth of which love alone is the absolute.

As human beings, we are not only ourselves. We are the country, in which we are born, the village, town, city, or farm, in which we grew up - and the place in which we learnt to walk, and the games we played, enjoyed, triumphed in and failed at. We are also the old folk and fairy tales we heard and read, the food we ate, and the schools and university we attended - and the sports we played or were excluded from. We are also that which we listened to, were taught, and the God we believed in. It is all these things and more that have made us what we are. These are things that you cannot come to know by hearsay. You can only know them by living them. You can only know them if you are them.

Journal Entry Number 1

AIDS Diary, New York City, 1986

The death of Elizabeth Taylor in 2011 brought it all back to me. The one and only time I spoke to her was to tell her that her friend and former dressmaker—Anthony Sofio—was dying of AIDS. She was immensely courteous and kind, sending Anthony the most beautiful bouquet of orchids I have ever seen. She wrote on the card: "To Dearest Anthony. I place my hand on your forehead and my head on your heart and wish you love. Elizabeth."

I remember that when I would tell these things to my straight friends or my work colleagues at Mount St Michael's Academy or my family back in Ireland, they tried hard to sympathise. Something was not right. It was as if they sensed that the experience was slowly and profoundly alienating me from them. This was more than the fact that I was working with the sick and dying. The awareness of the deaths of one's friends and the terrible sadness of the deep devastation, created a deep chasm between me and the rest of the world. The pain that I witnessed almost daily – not just the physical pain but all the psychological fear and homophobic shame that AIDS unleashed – all this was building an incubator that gradually shut most of my friends out of the deepest and most meaningful part of my life. One was either in or out. The two worlds did not mix.

There came a point at which the experience was so profound that it became impossible to talk about it. As I told less and less and experienced more and more, I found myself gravitating to those others who had experienced or were going through it as well. They were the ones who knew instinctively what I was feeling. These were the people to whom I did not have to explain over and again what I was going through. They knew with the knowledge of a lover, not simply the knowledge of a knower.

For a long time I did not break down or cry over any of the experiences of the Plague Years. I wanted to cry, but tears would not come for the friends, lovers and others to whom I ministered - all those whom I had known and loved and loved and known and who had gone and left me to go on. I was supposed to be the strong one. Sometimes it felt like I was carrying the burden of the whole world on my shoulders, and I could not take a step further. Then someone covered in Kaposi's sarcoma would come up to me and say, "Your presence gives me strength," and I would feel so ashamed. Who is the one who gives and who is the one who receives? I would ask myself.

I wanted to cry for Gustavo, the first one I knew to die of the 'gay plague' as it was called then. He left by his own hand in 1980 when no one knew what he had. Yes, I wanted to cry for Gerry, for Terry, and for Anne - for David, for Peter, and for Anthony - for Father's Declan, Philip Frank, and Father Jeremy - for David and Michael his partner - for young Michael, the first Irish guy I knew to be infected - for Keith, for Ernest, and for Thor - for Stephen, and for Jeff and Jimmy whose parents would not accept his ashes - for George and Tim, Red Tom and Bill - for Anthony and Rex - and for Ken and Kenny - for Brian, and for John, and for Peter - for Alan, for Colin, and for Hernando who took his own life - for Barry, for Martin, and for Roy - for Andy and for Joe - for Stephen and for Stewart - for Alistair and for Eamon especially - for John, for Jean Claude and for Sean - for Aldo the youngest one, a fourteen year old drug addict from the Bronx - for Roger, for Anthony and for Timothy - in London for Mark and John his young friend who took his own life, and for Colin - for Charles and John H., for Andrew - for David B., for Tiziano and for Kelvin – for Paul, for Alan, and for Steve and Michael, my Scottish friends and Celtic brothers - and of course for Ken Kitty a true hero – and for all the others I cannot remember - the hundreds of acquaintances to whom I had ministered. The friends who had died, and who I had mourned, or those whom I resisted mourning.

There were sudden flashes of panic at the thought of my own mortality that would send me into the woods of despair and I was lost. When Jeremy, my closest friend, mentor, professor, and former priest confessor died, the light went out in me. In that bitter poignant farewell my experience was totally denied, ignored, or simply not understood.

As Mark Halprin wrote in his novel, *A Soldier of the Great War*, "The war is still in him and will be in him for as long as he lives. For soldiers who have been bloodied are soldiers forever. We never fit in. That we cannot forget, that we do not forget, that we will never allow ourselves to heal completely, is our way of expressing our love for friends who have perished. We will not change because we have become what we have become to keep the fallen alive."

Early Spring

When I was eight years old, I was told that playing 'footsie' with the girl next door was wrong and shameful. 'Footsie' is a game children play, usually in spring or summertime. It consists simply of taking off one's shoes and socks, and sitting facing each other. Each player tries to push the other contestant with his or her bare feet. The one who succeeds in pushing the hardest usually wins. It is a simple, childish game and quite innocent. But this innocence was poisoned at the well of its own birth. I was not really sure why this was so. The invoking of 'telling the priest' if we did not put our shoes back on immediately on commencing a game of 'footsie' lodged in my young mind. There was something very wrong with flesh touching flesh.

Maybe my mother was having 'a bad day'. Nonetheless, the message landed indelibly on my soul. Sensual pleasure was wrong and against the priest and therefore God. This birth pang of Irish Jansenism and toxic shame has been the bane of my life. All pleasure is wrong. Sensual and sexual pleasure guarantees a hot and humid eternity. Despite twenty-five years of psychotherapy and much sexual experience, I still find it very difficult to connect my soul to my body in the act of making love to my lover and life partner with whom I have shared my life for more than eighteen years.

It is never too late to have a happy childhood, but I believe the 'brown paper bag' we inherit from our childhood profoundly affects our living and loving for the rest of our lives. While I am still Catholic and a priest, I don't know if the bag in which these two gifts were delivered has at times outweighed the beauty of the gift of faith—a gift that I cherish more than any other. The paradox is that it profoundly impairs the integration of my gay sexuality. I am far from alone in this. Many straight Catholic people I have seen for psychotherapy together with others of different religions or no religion, have likewise been warped by their religious enculturation and indoctrination.

The Word made flesh in the lives and loves of so many Christians has de facto been the Word made muck. This cannot be right from either a human or religious point of view. What is it one may well ask about our enfleshed desires that seems to frighten off so-called 'spiritual' people? Or the converse, what is it about the spirit or religious life that immediately seems to be antithetical to a life of human fleshy love? One would think that God having become human flesh in Christ is enough validation for us to be free to engage and enjoy relationships without all this policing of sexual desire which the Catholic Church in particular and other religious bodies in general are so notorious.

Sex can and does go wrong. So does every human activity, even that of the most noble and altruistic kind. Nevertheless, why does sex and pleasure receive such binding with briars throughout Christian history? To my mind, it is more than just a means of controlling people. It is certainly that. If one controls how those within a social group relate and breed, then that will most assuredly define everything from their economic to their private lives. There is a fear that if we take off the controls everyone will become an anarchist.

From the dawning of my own consciousness as a gay man, I have tried within the limitations of my humanity to seek the professional help to integrate my God-given sexuality with the rest of my humanity. As part of the process of engaging in that endeavour, I have also worked assiduously for lesbian, gay, transgendered and bisexual (LGTB) freedom. This struggle within me and outside of me has necessarily been at a certain cost. I realised very early on that anyone who goes after freedom from oppression, either for himself or for others, is going to be crucified. This was never more clear to me that in the midst of the AIDS holocaust in New York City in the 1980s. As hundreds of our friends and associates died around us, we fell out of our closets and took to the streets to seek protection in jobs and housing for our most vulnerable sisters and brothers. It was as Dickens wrote about another revolutionary era "the best of times and the worst of times."

There was very little time to think; what was needed was action. People were sick and dying and being ignored by the church and by state authorities. Worse still, our gay brothers were being blamed for their illness. The first statement from the Vatican by a then Monsignor, now Archbishop Foley was: "AIDS is the natural result of unnatural acts." Such outrageous rhetoric would never be used in the context of other diseases. The most obvious been the clear and scientifically based link between cancer and smoking.

I went to City Hall in New York in 1986 to testify before the city council for the passage of 'Intro. 2'. This bill was put forward to guarantee lesbians and gays protection against discrimination in jobs and housing and had been defeated in Council for fifteen years running. Justice demanded that, its passage in the light of the AIDS crisis in our midst was an absolute necessity. People with AIDS and their partners, had already been thrown out of their apartments and fired from their jobs. Its chief opponent was the Archdiocese of New York, which used all of its political muscle to force Catholic politicians to vote against the bill. John Cardinal O' Connor led the opposition with his infamous line of attack: "God's law cannot be changed." How the Cardinal succeeded in mangling God's law into discrimination against a struggling and now dying minority I shall never know. On hearing of the Church's opposition and being steeped in ministry to people suffering and dying, I joined the struggle for justice and testified for the bill. The bill finally passed. But the battle had just begun.

In 1984 my closest priest friend and former professor and confessor died of complications related to HIV/AIDS. He had been working at the school in which I was Campus Minister for over six years. On his death, his brother and fellow priest started a witch-hunt at the school to have me ousted from my position. In some crazy way, he blamed me for his beloved brother's death. He arrived at the school several times with placards denouncing me publicly as an 'avowed homosexual' and a 'danger to the students.'

At the particular time, I was theological consultant to Dignity/New York, an organisation for the pastoral and social support of lesbian and gay Catholics. As with all gay organisations in the city, the AIDS pandemic was having a devastating effect on our membership. As one of the priests involved with the community, I was naturally and necessarily deeply committed to care for those ill and dying. While this particular work was enervating and challenging, it did not interfere with my duties as campus minister to Mount St. Michael's Academy in the Bronx. Although my superiors were aware of my involvement, they had no difficulty with it. In fact, many of my colleagues both admired and supported my work. I was out as a gay man to all of my friends, but not in the school to my pupils or most of my colleagues.

When my sexual orientation came into the public forum during the witch-hunt, there was initially no outcry. The principal of the school remained silent, but not for long. Three teachers in the school joined in the witch-hunt and went to the principal demanding my resignation. I was summoned to the principal's office and told that I would have to go. I protested my complete innocence and told the authorities that in no way would I be scape-goated in this fashion. I was also pertinently aware that the principal was himself gay and had been seen by many of my friends in Dignity in gay bars in the city. Eventually 'for the good of the school', I agreed to resign and was given a full year's salary with excellent references. The principal died of AIDS-related illness two years later.

I took advantage of my forced resignation to throw myself headlong into my pastoral ministry with those in our community suffering and dying. The Archdiocese of New York was not at all happy and would not renew my faculties (licence) to minister as a priest. I tried several other bishops, but everywhere I went I was blackballed.

Eventually, my religious superiors were forced by Cardinal O'Connor to order me to Rome. My stay there, although orchestrated by the Congregation of the Doctrine of the Faith (formerly known as the Inquisition) led by Cardinal Joseph Ratzinger (now Pope Benedict XVI), was pleasant enough. I stayed in the headquarters of the community to which I belonged, the Society of African Missions (S.M.A.), and studied French and Marian spirituality at the Angelicum and Gregorian Universities. I was ordered by Cardinal Ratzinger to be faithful to Church teachings in my ministry. Subsequently I had to sign a document to that effect. I had no difficulty in so doing as I made clear to my own superiors. Pursuing justice for the oppressed and caring for the sick and dying was to my mind the most sacred duty the Church had in light of the Gospel of Jesus Christ.

In Rome, I made contact with the local HIV/AIDS support groups for gay men. I was shocked, but not surprised, to learn that there was no support whatsoever from any of the thousands of church bodies in Rome. I invited members of the support groups to a Mass and social at my religious society's headquarters. They expressed their hurt and anger at the Church and deep-felt gratitude for our hospitality. As I learned, there was little in the way of an open gay community in the Eternal City. Everything was underground and buried in shame and secrecy. There was lots of sex available, but few bars or centres in which people could meet and form loving and lasting relationships. Undoubtedly, this was a direct consequence of the Catholic Church's unrelenting condemnation and oppression of gay people. 'Don't humanise your sexuality' is the unspoken but unquestionable message of the Church to sexual minorities. The very same Church that condemns gay men for sexual promiscuity fosters it in every single utterance from its magisterium.

While in Rome, Cardinal O'Connor in New York was making sure that I would not return. Together with the help of the FBI and an organisation called SAFE (Students Against Faggots in Education) at my former school, the witch-hunt took on a new momentum. The FBI with the New York City police vice squad started an investigation of 'certain goings on' that had been reported to them by 'concerned church authorities' and some teachers. At first, my name did not surface in the investigation. I had already been out of the school for four years. Eventually when my name was mentioned, a seventeen year-old student claimed under coercive pressure and unethical tactics by the investigating agent, that I had molested him as a fourteen year-old.

I was on retreat in Dublin preparing for my return to HIV/AIDS ministry in New York when I received the word from my Provincial in Cork, Ireland that the FBI was looking for me. I had absolutely no idea why. I was not left in the dark for long. Subsequently, after some excellent legal advice paid for by my religious community, I returned to New York in a hail of lurid tabloid publicity to face the charges brought against me.

At the time, I was given very little hope of justice. After all, I was up against two of the most powerful institutions in the world: the Roman Catholic Church and the Federal Bureau of Investigation. For almost an entire calendar year, together with my defence team and loyal friends, I went back and forth to the Bronx Supreme Court to try to clear my name of these outrageous and calumnious charges.

Eventually at trial on 21 April 1989, my accuser, John Schaefer, refused to testify. Having admitted that he had been forced against his will to bring the charges by Special Agent McDonald, he refused to go further with the case. Schaefer was nineteen years of age at the time. The judge, Justice Burton Roberts, not only dismissed the charges and berated the politically motivated prosecutors from the District Attorney's office, but dramatically and fiercely declared me wholly innocent.

It was a pyrrhic victory. The effects of this soul murder by the Church I served and devoted my life to in New York will follow me to the grave. After the trial, I could no longer work for the Church. I remained in priestly ministry and continued my pastoral care for people who were HIV positive. Eventually I felt I had to get out of the city in which I had made a home dearer to me than any other I had known and I immigrated to London. At least, I thought to myself, if I get away from all the politics and publicity for a while, maybe I can then return and start anew. I was wrong. Little did I think on arrival in London in the spring of 1992 that here my life would change utterly from anything I had previously known. All of my adolescence and during my young adult life I had dreamt of some day meeting someone with whom I could share a life of lasting love.

Journal Entry Number 2

In order to pursue my doctoral studies - 1977 to1980 - I had to find a position to support myself financially. The parish of Saint Gabriel's in the North West Bronx, where I was associate pastor from 1975 to 1978 could not do this. In fact, the pastor was seriously opposed to my pursuing my doctoral studies at New York Theological non-Catholic Seminary. "I don't want any priest of mine attending Protestant seminary and preaching Protestant theology to my people."

I had completed my Master's degree - within the fold - at the Jesuits' Fordham University Lincoln Center campus in Manhattan. Consequently, I sought and found employment at Mount Saint Michael's Academy, a high school owned and operated by the Marist Brothers of the Schools in the North East Bronx. The Brothers supported my studies and allowed me the necessary time to complete them. Meanwhile at Saint Gabriel's parish where I was popular with those of a more liberal persuasion, there was much sadness tempered with a little anger and hurt that I was being forced to move elsewhere to do my academic work. This is my farewell address to the group I founded for the study of psychology and theology at Saint Gabriel's in 1976. The group is still in existence to this very day, albeit in a different form.

Farewell St. Gabriel's, 9 May 1978

There is loneliness in the heart of each one of us that is never overcome. As I have often said in other contexts, the fascination and bitterness of sexual experience lies precisely here. Sexual congruence points to a total sharing that cannot be realised in this time called life. It is in that sense a true sacrament of what is and what is not.

Aloneness has so much to do with Christ's message to us. We Christians are lonely by the very fact of belonging to him and the more we seek to follow him, strangely the more does our loneliness increase. There are anguishing experiences of not belonging, either to this world or to the next – not being able to explain the existential loneliness we are experiencing – even while being in the midst of people.

Sometimes we think all that we need is closeness to a person we love. Sometimes it seems as though physical closeness might answer the need. Sometimes our hearts are so full of confusion, so filled with our own tears, while in our faces people who are not too sensitive think they see contentment. We all know these feelings. Yet often it is when we are at our lowest ebb that God is closest to us. The truth is that Christ thought that in his twelve apostles he had an understanding community, yet in the Garden of Gethsemane He was alone. He too asked, indeed He sought, the Father God to take away the absolute and absurd pain of His loneliness.

We cannot cope with human life on the human level alone. For anyone who has had even a glimpse of the Absolute understands this. Knowing God, even for the briefest instant, creates a hunger that is often incredibly painful. The only way to assuage it that I know of is by continuing in prayer and reflection, even against all odds. For to love is a decision, it is not simply a feeling. Each one of us, in different and diverse ways, experiences the wilderness situation. Like Abraham and Jeremiah, we know that God has at some time addressed us. Now He is the silent God. He seems not to be responding. All we can do is continue to wander in the darkness, in the direction we think He wants us to go.

At times that God whom we have tried to so love and who first loved us, does nothing to lift our burdens or to lighten our darkness. He is not at our beck and call. There is in fact a rhythm of presence and absence, of word and silence, of infinite loneliness, when the God to whom we felt so close at one time becomes radical mystery. At this very point in our experience, I believe we are growing as never before. We do not lead one another to God as a result of sharing a wonderful feeling of His presence. We lead one another to Him most of all when we struggle across an infinite remoteness, in doubt and fear, in shame and guilt, but also in wonder and mystery, conversation and joy.

At one time or another we all live with heart breaking in the wilderness situation. Then we tend to think of our God as unknowing and uncaring. I believe with all of my heart that in these times when we call out to Him and seem to get no answer at all, He is in fact listening most intently. It is in these winters that the real meaning of faith, hope, and love are given birth. We must spend much time in labour before we give birth to God in us.

We really need each other to share our pain and loneliness when we are experiencing this seemingly unknowing God. We all experience it at times. Even those who have never known God experience it in the painful and often terrifying meaninglessness of their lives. We do not tell others about it, because in fact it is a mystery. We go ahead in quiet desperation believing in the God who does not exist for us.

Your future, like your past, has to be bought, fought for, and won by your personal responsibility in the face of mystery. Our desperate hope is so often expressed in the simple words, "O God I can take no more." This silent, incomprehensible mystery of God engulfs our living and our dying, in fact our entire pilgrimage through the world. Yet even here, we can be a presence of God to our fellow human beings. This is one of the most extraordinary experiences I have had in my own life: while my own soul cried out in desperation for the comfort of God, I could and have been a comfort to others. This in itself is an answer. It seems that what God wants of us is not that we feel like petted children, safe and secure, but that we become for our sisters and brothers a promiscuity of grace, unique, irreplaceable, and charismatically individual. He or She can empower us to transcend ourselves and touch the other. This to me seems to be what all true love is.

We must go through our pain and loneliness and yet keep telling others of the wonder and mystery of him for whom we ache in longing. This time alone in the image of a lonely God will be a time when our hearts are broken for love. Knowledge of God gradually penetrates all other knowledge. In the darkness we are often strangely nearest the light. The longing, which so often expresses itself in our present unhappiness, cries out to be expressed and shared with each other. Our personal weaknesses are part of the deep struggle with which He blesses those who want to live like Christ. Such personal weaknesses, like those of Job and Lear, keep us open and humble. We can never claim to have the answers, but we do come to know and understand the questions.

Spring

In classical Freudian psychology, an absent father and close-binding mother is the supposed recipe for a homosexual. Like all fathers of my generation, my father had to work all the hours God sent to keep his family fed and clothed. Consequently, growing up in the 1950s I did not see a lot of him. My mother ran and managed the home and rarely ventured outside of it, except to shop for our needs. It is true to say she was the home and, as a child, it was inconceivable and unimaginable to be home without her. But that is the home that all my brothers and sisters grew up in. I turned out to be gay and they heterosexual. I believe that children are born gay or straight or bisexual as the case may be—that our sexual orientations are innate and natural to us.

From the dawn of my sexual awareness, I remember being attracted to my own gender. When at five years of age the boy next door suggested we play Cowboys and Indians, I insisted we play Indians only so that we could run around our back yard naked as I imagined Indians did in the Wild West. West Clare was wild but not ready for my version of 'going native'. My mother put a quick end to our shenanigans by suddenly appearing for a bucket of coal. From that earliest memory and the next forty years of my life, I would seek and search for a boy and then a man to love and live with, in the same way straight people do for a person of the opposite gender. Little did I realise at the time that such a desire and deep human need was criminal, sick, and sinful in the land of my birth. Even though I would spare no price and count no cost in my search, I would not find such love and companionship for almost fifty years.

Every boy I knew as a child became my pal. There is nothing unique about that. I am well aware that such peer relationships are usually affectionate and intimate without being in any way sexual. As a gay boy I knew that, even though relatively popular with the others, I did not fit in. I was not good at games and overcompensated by concentrating on my running ability to the exclusion of all other sports, apart from swimming. Even as a child, I was fascinated by opera and musicals. I became an altar boy at the age of eight. As well as allowing me to dress up in my soutane and starched white surplice, I was able to learn all the church music and sing along with the Cathedral choir.

Gregorian chant and Palestrina Masses were the meat and potatoes of every Catholic Church in those pre-Vatican II days. Latin was the language of the liturgy and music. My father taught me the responses and I fell head over heels in love with the theatricality and campness of it all. I was the best little altar boy in the world. I rarely missed an opportunity to serve High Mass, Low Mass, Benediction, Rosary, or Stations of the Cross. The liturgy of the day was pure Broadway. This was most obviously so during the seasons of Easter and Christmas. The sacristan's favourite altar boys would get the big parts. I always succeeded in getting a principal role and consequently was in my holy element.

It was on the altar stage that I first learnt the transparent attractiveness of being in front of an audience and playing a role. This served me for both good and ill throughout most of my life. The altar boy's dress, and the priest's later, provided me with an escape from my true God-given nature. It was and is a good one, but results in a dangerous and damaging splitting of the human psyche. As I got closer to God, I got further away from myself. While running around the sanctuary of Ennis Cathedral as an altar boy, I was pertinently aware that I wanted and desired at the deepest level of my humanity to be both affectionately and physically close to the other boys. No matter how hard I tried to suppress these feelings, their prevenient persistence never eluded me. I did not act out on them until much later with two older boys and then the trouble began.

Sick, sinful, and against human nature is how my first confessor at age eleven described them. "Jesus, I'm damned," I thought. I tried every devotion and novena known to the pious Catholic world, together with regular Holy Mass, Confession and Holy Communion to suppress my feelings of same-sex attraction, but all to no avail. Such suppression and repression lead only to obsession. While for a period of some years after my first sexual experience with two older boys I did succeed in foregoing sexual activity, nothing or no one could stop me from 'falling in love'. This happened for the first time when I was sixteen years of age.

I fell head over heels in love with my best friend. This was completely, utterly, and totally different from 'feeling up' another boy, as we called it. In fact, the first time I was 'felt up' by the boy four years my senior; I was given a holy picture of Saint Theresa for allowing him to touch me. This only worked until he ran out of holy pictures. With my best friend there were no bribes. There was no sexual activity. On my part there was the deepest need simply to hold hands with the hope that maybe we could or would kiss at some time. I realised that this was anathema in our world, and still is in Catholic circles. The institutional Church can forgive us in the confessional for having sex. What it cannot tolerate is a lifestyle of love and devotion – like heterosexual marriage - in which sexual activity plays a part. Women and men who are lesbian or gay and who are in lifelong committed relationships are according to Catholic teaching "living in sin."

My best friend was indeed a good friend and did show affection and love for me. He was not in love with me. I was besotted with him. This was tolerable until he turned his affections to a girl we both liked. I immediately of course said I was attracted and interested in her girlfriend. I wasn't. I felt I had to 'play it straight' or lose him completely. I went through the charade of going out with this girl for some time. She was very attractive both physically and personally. Kissing her for me was like kissing a post. It did nothing for me but filled me with guilt and shame at my deceitfulness.

What else could I do? My best friend and I would double date.

As I watched him kiss his sweetheart, I would dissolve into floods of tears and try to explain to my girlfriend that it was my first time being in love. She thought it was with her. I could not find the words to say that he was the one for whom my heart ached. He was the one I thought about first thing in the morning and last thing at night. He was the one with who I longed to be, to touch, to hold, to kiss, to live, and to love all my life days long. It was impossible. It was excruciatingly painful. Every time I sought counsel from a priest, I was reduced to sin. My love and longings were sin. I was a pervert. I had one of two choices: find the right girl or explore a vocation to priesthood or religious life.

'Finding the right girl' was the general advice given in confession when one admitted to homosexual activity. Very often, this advice resulted in homosexual men or women marrying and having children while remaining more sexually attracted toward their own gender. I have had countless experiences of this in my work as a priest and psychotherapist. Never was the sin of the Church so inhuman than when some of these married men caught the HIV/AIDS virus in the early days of the pandemic and passed it on to their beloved wives. These men had struggled with their sexuality all their lives. While remaining faithful to their marriage vows as best they could, their repression now resulted in death for them as well as their spouses.

Sexuality is much more fluid than was originally thought. We are capable of sexual relations with opposite or same gender partners. Most people do have a preference. It is not just lust. It is the way we fall in love. To force a woman or man into a sexual relationship with someone to whom she or he is not sexually attracted is utterly wrong, both psychosexually and morally. This was quite common up until recent times. For myself, I knew in my heart of hearts that I was not sexually attracted to women. Although the words gay and homosexual were never heard, I knew I was different. Marriage to a woman was not an option.

I opted for the Church and decided to become a priest. No one in my family or circle of friends was surprised to hear this at the time. After all, I had been a pious little creep from as long as I can remember. How many little boys do you know who accepted holy pictures for sexual favours as a kid? Or indeed sold holy books for the Legion of Mary, while most of my friends played hurling or football on Saturday afternoon.

Books like 'The Devil at Dances', 'What a Boy Should Know', 'What a Girl Should Know' polluted our young minds with shame and guilt in regard to everything sexual. In primary school, the Dominic Savio Club, which we were all encouraged to join to protect our holy purity, forbade us to look at the screen while at the local Gaiety Cinema if a man and woman kissed each other. This was the public moral stance preached, while the principal of the same school 'felt up' the good-looking students as he helped them out with their school lessons. In sixth form, as one of my classmates said to me most recently, we were caught between being sexually abused by the Brother in charge and risking being mercilessly beaten for the slightest provocation or failure by his opposite number on the lay faculty. As I look back on both my primary and secondary school education in Ennis, I regard myself lucky to be half-normal. Brutality reigned supreme and left an indelible mark on my soul and every bone in my body.

In fourth grade, I still remember my two closest friends being asked by the lay teacher to hold my right hand and left hand respectively. He named them 'Gardaí' after the Irish police force. He then proceeded to slap me across the face for not knowing the correct answer to a simple mathematical question. I have naturally dreaded this same subject ever since. While studying for my Masters in psychology years later, I had to get special tuition for a class in statistics, as the very thought of dealing with numbers sent me into paroxysms of terror...

When I left Ennis Christian Brothers School after eleven years and boarded the train for Cloughballymore, Co. Galway to commence my training for priesthood, I felt as if I had completed a jail sentence. The goodness of some teachers and the education I received was completely overshadowed by the atmosphere of brutality and psycho-emotional abuse. Ironically, the Brother who most sexually abused us was also the Brother who gave us most educationally. He introduced operetta to the school. He was also responsible for gymnastics and beautiful drill displays that took place in the town sports field every year.

I starred in the school opera as I was a talented boy soprano. This early introduction to the stage at the age of eleven boosted my ratings amongst my peers and compensated for my being "fuckin' useless", as my friends would say, at hurling and football.

Journal Entry Number 3

Every year for as far back as I can remember our family made their annual pilgrimage to Lahinch for a week or two holidays by the Atlantic Ocean. This gift was unique. No one else in our neighbourhood that I knew of could afford such luxury. The truth is we could ill afford it ourselves. My parents denied themselves and made what I now consider heroic sacrifices from the 1950s onwards so that their children could be educated and once a year enjoy a stay in this most beautiful seaside resort on Europe's most western seaboard. I have the happiest memories of such times. We returned to Ennis after our holidays with Lahinch accents and what sun, wind, and rain could provide in colouring our skin to prove that we had been away on holiday by the sea.

As I grew older, I always wanted a place of my own near Lahinch. Eventually when I had enough money, my father and mother helped me make my dream come through and found for me what I can only describe as my little piece of heaven on this earth. Slí Eile, Barrtrá is that place. When the well-known writer and broadcaster Nuala O'Faolain bought the house up the bótharín from me and moved there with her wife, Nell McCafferty, I thought God had indeed smiled on the place.

Memories of Nuala, 30 May 2008

When I was a child and our family came to Lahinch, there weren't nearly as many houses or people as there are now. The geography of the village and the singularity of the sea were far more noticeable then. We were different. Kids were different. It took us longer to understand the things we felt. There was certain inevitability that as soon as I could I would have my own plot of land near here. It was, I suppose, the totemic connectedness I felt to the earth and sea from which I was made, in this place. That is how I met Nuala. She bought the house of the late Miss Mary Shannon from whom I had purchased my plot in 1977.

At that time, I was teaching as a priest in New York City. New York being irredeemably hot in July and August, I would invariably come back to Barrtrá to get away from the heat and to see my family and friends. Nell – Nuala's wife at the time – was the first to visit the old trailer I had on the site. In the duty-free shop at Kennedy Airport on the way to Shannon, I would purchase liquor, and later she would help me polish it off.

Gradually at first and then more, in fact, after her break up with Nell, Nuala and I formed our own relationship. She had a real interest in the work I did with young gay men dying of HIV and AIDS in New York. This was very much borne out when in Easter of 2007 she invited me, Billy my partner and some friends, to bless her newly renovated house in Barrtrá, even though she had little respect for "that all male priesthood to which you belong."

Teach us to number our days aright
That we may gain wisdom of heart

So the psalmist prays in one of my favourite psalms, Psalm 90. If I were to sum up what I knew of Nuala O'Faolain in a sentence, it would be that: Wisdom of heart. Not the wisdom of the knower – although she had much knowledge – but the wisdom of the lover. Time is on the side of those who love. Only those who love can touch the meaning of time, which in its profoundest significance is always time of meeting, of encounter, of being with and for others, of shared and received presence. Yes, in life she touched the meaning of time because she touched so many with her words and work. Through her art – writing and broadcasting – she performed the task of the lover so well. The artist and lover are one. If I love you, I shall teach you things you do not know.

First of all, Nuala loved life. I can still see her casually walking down the bótharín in Barrtrá with her dog Molly or later Mabel. Or, skipping over the rocks for an afternoon, she would swim, in one of the rock pools, when the tide was in. For Nuala, as she often told me, to breathe the air there, simply to be, was itself a glorious thing. She knew that life itself, existence itself, was the most precious thing we know, that life is grace to us, our own lives, and the lives of those around us, that all things great and small are gifts. There are treasures that we can at any moment discover and a banquet to which we are all equally invited. For Nuala, as I knew her, the true value of all that exists was discovered in the way one values a gift. She cherished life and existence and especially other people who listened to her words and read her writings, and so enabled them to discover the treasure hidden in their own lives.

When on 24 March – Easter Monday 2008 – I saw her for the last time, Nuala was in despair. I had heard she was seriously ill while I was visiting my father in Ennis. Without waiting to be invited, I was determined to see her. I was not prepared for what I saw. Her friend Helen announced to Nuala that "your neighbour, priest-friend is here to see you." Nuala on my entrance greeted me with, "none of that priest stuff, Bernárd" . . ."there is no God for me" . . . and then immediately "What am I going to do? Tell me what was it like working and accompanying all those young men you saw dying of HIV and AIDS?" I was speechless and deeply troubled. I muttered something like, "Nuala, all I have is my faith—my hope, if you will, that there is something more than this. If I did not, as Camus would say, 'I would have killed myself long ago'. It's a hope Nuala without proof, that there is Another Country . . . Most people call it God . . . Something happens to your heart when you are open to the possibility of God . . ." I could say no more. I had already said too much. I would never see her again in this time called life.

Yet, time and eternity is on the side of those who love. I believe Nuala loved and loved much. Yes, we all know that she had lifelong difficulty in believing she was loved by anybody - her family, friends, and even her partner, John. True to the very end, she was teaching us how little time there is for any of us. There is so much to be done; so many need our love and there is so little time.

I cannot promise myself tomorrow. I only have today. Only today am I alive to live and to love. We cannot wait for tomorrow, for tomorrow the other may be dead. In the wisdom of Nuala's heart, she knew the importance of the 'now' in human living. This was not that each moment should be a frantic search for meaning and for goodness, for wholeness in word and work. Therein madness lies. Concisely, a simple awareness that life is what matters, and its images are here and now – in this suffering, in this joy, in this person. Today is important, for salvation is now, love is now, and life is now.

As Leo Tolstoy, the Russian philosopher, novelist and poet wrote:

> The most difficult thing
> But an essential one
> Is to love life,
> To love it even while one suffers,
> Because life is all. Life is God
> And to love life is to love God.

Nothing, from the first day I saw her and no one thing that has happened to me since, has ever been as frightening and as confusing. For few women I have ever known have ever done more to make me more certain and more insecure, more important and less significant.

Yes, as Yeats had it (to paraphrase his Broken Dreams . . .):

> Vague memories, nothing but memories
> But in the grave all, all, shall be renewed.

The certainty that I shall see this woman
Leaning or standing or walking
In the first loveliness of her youth
And with the burning fervour of her youthful eyes,
Has set me muttering like a fool.

Yes, people of Nuala's and my generation were different then. Life was different. It took us longer to understand the things we felt . . . and yet we learnt . . .

Life is full of comings and goings
And for everything we take with us
There is something we leave behind

There will always be very special piece of Nuala O'Faolain in Lahinch/Barrtrá. I trust that there is a special piece of Lahinch/Barrtrá where Nuala is now.

Nuala, Slán go fóill
Nuala, Goodbye for now.

Late Spring

One may well ask if leaving secondary school and deciding to enter a religious novitiate at age seventeen was in fact stepping out of the frying pan into the fire. Yes and no. A gay boy at seventeen in rural communities is usually doing all he can to cover what he is. This of course is usually aided and abetted by Church and society. At least this was the case in most societies up until very recently. Entering the priesthood for me, while fulfilling my heart's desire at one level, also gave me the perfect cover and acceptance that I longed for—at least unconsciously.

The aching longing for physical closeness to another male was always there, but was never articulated in childhood, adolescence or young adulthood except through a series of intimate and very often deeply spiritual friendships. When physical desire became visible, the encounter was always awkward and, if sexual, usually nothing more than 'touchy feely' groping that often resulted in later years in mutual masturbation. This of course was always followed by enormous guilt and shame and the resolve in confession to never to do it again.

Frequent confession became the vehicle of sexual arrested development. When asked by a Franciscan friar in Ennis if I ever touched myself or another boy or girl, I told him in all innocence that, "yes I touched another boy my own age." I was told by the priest, for what sounded like the umpteenth time, that this was "a serious sin against nature". I felt then as I do now that sexual congress with a consenting male was my nature, although of course I could not articulate it as such at the time.

Father Cyril went into the most lurid detail, asking totally inappropriate questions about what I did and did not do. He made a sexual Inquisition out of what should have been a pastoral sacramental experience of God's love. He was of course stimulating himself at my expense. He continued this abuse by insisting I return to him weekly to confess any thoughts, desires, words or deeds I would have against holy purity. I was to identify myself on entering the confession box by greeting him with the words, "I come to you Father." This was in contrast to the regular prescribed formula: "Bless me Father for I have sinned." Years later, while awaiting family from Ireland at New York Kennedy Airport, I ran into an old friend of mine from Ennis who greeted me with the words, "I come to you Father." He too had been a victim of Father Cyril's voyeurism. This and too many other incidents of Church-related emotional and psychosexual denigration left my gay soul in a very sick state. While I understand and accept that at the time the culture and historical context was very different, that is no excuse for the brutalisation of the young and vulnerable.

Journal Entry Number 4

The homilies and talks shared here were given at either Masses or public occasions for the lesbian, gay, bisexual and transgendered Catholic community and their straight friends. In many ways, it is more difficult to 'come out' to people as Catholic than it is as lesbian or gay. People generally in my experience cannot understand or accept why a persecuted and defamed sexual minority would want to belong to a church that is both the cause and the means to our persecution and defamation.

Nowhere is this as true as in Ireland. As Tonie Walsh - a gay rights leader in Dublin - said when presenting me with the Hirschfeld Award for my work with the LGBT community in 1986, "Our problem with you Bernárd is you make the Catholic Church look good." Twenty-three years later, when invited to speak at the annual carol service for LGBT people and our friends, much had changed in the land of my birth. Yet the struggle was still on for full and equal recognition of our marriages of love.

Made in God's Lesbian/Gay Image
Dublin, 12 December 2009

I am indeed honoured to be invited to speak to you this evening. I am grateful to my host - Brian Glennon - for the invitation and the gracious hospitality afforded me and my husband, Billy Lynch-Desmond.

As lesbian, gay, bisexual and transgendered people - together with our straight friends - we have the responsibility of a special spiritual calling. We have known our experience of the human erotic possibility to be both Bethlehem and Calvary: Bethlehem, in that we are created and born as the gay/lesbian image of God: Calvary in that our birth robs us of our birthright, our absolute right to live and love as co-equals in our families, churches, towns, villages, and the country of our birth is unalienable. We have found both the joy of finding love and the persecution of our performances of love. Moreover, we know that one of the primary persecutors has been organised religion within which many of us found our origins in faith.

We believe that we have been inspired by the Holy Spirit to create various occasions of witness to who we are and how we love in history. From the Hirschfeld Centre to GLEN (Gay/Lesbian, Equality Network), the Irish Gay Rights Movement to the National Gay Federation, to Noise (Campaign for Civil Marriage), and this carol service - all these and many more groups and individuals have been such occasions of inspiring witness of the Spirit of God alive and well in our midst. We know that whatever organised religion may say, our way of loving is as an essential part of the Body of Christ/God as any other form of sexual or spiritual love. Each of us has had to make the journey over many trials and doubts to the confident resolution that it is love, alive in the soul and, indeed, sacramentally expressed with our bodies, which is the appearance of God. No holy communion is more holy than the human communion of two people in love.

Neither God nor love can be limited in their infinite sway to any particular performance of sexuality. I believe we can honestly assert that the oppression and repression of human sexual fulfilment is the primary cause of sickness in our communities, straight and gay. We know, in our heart of hearts, that our love sexually expressed is not sin. If we are to ensure that our exploration of how our love might most be a search for God, then it is important that we name our love as grace – gift of God – in all its many and varied forms. (HIV/AIDS I have always believed - from my many years of work in the field primarily with Gay men - is a disease contacted primarily in the search for Love, the search for touch, the search for Life and God.)

This does not mean that love and sex cannot go wrong. They can and do, as do all human endeavours no matter how noble their aspiration or godlike their ideal. Human sexual expression will always fall short of the ideal, precisely because it points to a total sharing that cannot be realised in this time called life. That is why the French call sexual orgasm 'le petit mort' – the little death. Human, loving sexual expression is always a kind of sacrament that leaves us wanting more and pointing to something/someone beyond ourselves.

Our spiritual quest within how we love continues to present a radical challenge to both Church and State. On the one hand, it indeed has been our experience that whatever may be anyone's individual preference for lesbian/gay marriage - and I am one married gay man - such definitions of relationship do not complete the description of what might be good and whole expressions of love and God. We know that finding attractiveness in another human being and acting from this recognition – both occasions of God's grace – have many variations and possibilities. We are right to declare that our responsible, non-exploitative explorations of these many possibilities and forms of relationship constitute the full potential of loving as a gift. We offer this to human society. In our actions and sometimes our sufferings, we give witness to the wrongness of patriarchal, heterosexist prescription of human erotic liberation. This is a serious and complex challenge we present to society, our Church, and ourselves. Nevertheless, we believe that God lives in love and that in fact God's love – as the celebration of Christmas bears witness – is Love made Flesh, with all its precariousness, vulnerability and transparent volatility.

There are times in our own imperfect lives when the veil parts between the two worlds we contain - our inner desire for a more divine destiny and the hard reality of our present circumstances. In 'Postscript', Seamus Heaney writes about the "sideways breeze off the ocean that catches us off guard and blows our heart wide open." Such sacramental glimpses have an edge to them, blessing us forever. Brian Friel's play Dancing at Lúnasa, for example, features five sexually frustrated sisters in their County Donegal cottage in 1936. It is the time of the annual Celtic harvest festival named after the pagan god Lú. Things are not good. Disgrace and penury are killing their stifled souls. Dancing is the key metaphor of the play. In a most extraordinary burst of energy, the five women release their emotional and sexual suppression by dancing to a reel issuing from their new-fangled wireless. It is a glimpse of unquenchable passions that comes from far beyond words. There are many ways of having such small epiphanies of the underlying reality of our lives.

Because God is not what we think She is, Her Spirit finds us where and when we least expect it. The exchange of Christmas cards and greetings at this time of year, remind us anew that friendship is one of the truest faces of God. Or is there anything more godlike, than the transparent beauty of a child's joy on discovering what Santa has brought? Beyond a passing celebration of Christmas, this way of being in the world is a daily participation in Incarnation; it is God made flesh living. This is Advent time, and it is always a time of waiting for God to make love to us in different and diverse people and places. We are perennially called to be God's mystics as we search for God's traces everywhere: diviners who detect the holy water of life in the earth of our being.

These almost subliminal but breathtaking glimpses are all tiny incarnations of heaven's promise that "Between God and us there is no between" (Eckhart). Without them we forget and lose the way "the way of truly seeing" (Daniel Berrigan). R.S. Thomas calls it in, The Bright Field, 'The turning aside like Moses to the miracle of the lit bush, to a brightness that seemed as transitory as your youth once, but is the eternity that awaits you."

Whether it be the wild dance across the fields of Ballybeg, in Brian Freel's Dancing at Lúnasa. The human communion made holy in the body of a lover. The countless daily graces that enable us to see into and beyond the immediate reality, transcending and transforming it into a new creation. These are all sustained and intensified by that enduring night, when God's astonishing desire to be partnered with us was revealed and concealed in the baby of Bethlehem. This God-child, who was made flesh for us, in the flesh and blood, sweat and semen, of our own attempts to love each other as LGTB and straight people.

It is good to be a seeker. Gay people have a particular nadir to seek the best, to go after the best, to give generously of their best. While seeking out the God and goodness of life and love is necessary, eventually we have to become finders and give the gift we have found into the world. To my mind, this is our moment to give the world, the Church, the State publicly and proudly our love. As Henri Nouwen, a gay brother and theologian, so eloquently put it: "the real conversion is the un-covering of the truth that it is safe to love." This is what binds us, love. This is both sacred and playful. For love is above all playful like Lady Wisdom in the Book of Proverbs. As a people with an in-depth awareness of our own spirituality we know it is safe for us to be vulnerable to each other, to be available to each other, to surrender to each other, to suffer with each other. "Love and do what you will," Saint Augustine tells us.

It is preposterous and an outrage against all of humanity that any two people have to ask to have their love recognised by the laws of the land. Our love for each other as couples is second to none. We are not better than heterosexual couples, but nor are we less than heterosexuals when we commit to live in covenants of love. Marriage and adoption are our right as a people co-equally made in the image and likeness of God. We are not asking for favours or special treatment. We are simply saying as Irish citizens, our lives and our loves are as much part of what it is to be Irish, what it is to be human, what it is to be in God as any and every person born on this island. Our fight for that right is a work of love not only for ourselves, but also for all people – especially our gay and lesbian children who shall come after us - and who like us will desire to live here in freedom, happiness and peace. We must wear our continued struggle for the freedom to love as a badge of honour and belongingness to the God who is love. A God whose birth and becoming one of us we celebrate at this time.

Beanneachtaí na Féile libh agus gach rath don Athbhlian.

Merry Christmas and Happy New Year.

Early Summer

My first experience of being in an environment of hope was my year in the house of formation of the Society of African Missions, in Cloughballymore, Kilcolgan, Co. Galway. There were twenty-six of us from all over Ireland and three from England. We ranged in age from seventeen to thirty years of age. Most of us were teenagers. Some of the boys had been to Juniorate at the African Missions secondary school in Ballinafad, County Mayo. We were quite a mixed bunch and for the most part full of the joys of our new found vocation as student priests. We were met at Ardrahan railway station by a farm steward, Mr Cohen, and the priest in charge of the farm at our house of formation. We piled into the back of farm trucks, with our luggage in tow and headed for ten months of aesthetical theology and preparation for priesthood. We looked like boy priests as we donned the clerical soutane and Roman collar for the first time.

Before leaving for the noviciate, my parents had travelled with me to Cleary's, a large clothing department store in Dublin, to outfit me for my new state in life. My mother had not been to Dublin since her honeymoon, eighteen years earlier. With six young children to feed, I being the first-born, trips away from home, as already stated was not an indulgence easily entertained. This excursion to Dublin was a major event—and a major expense for my family. Yet my parents were so proud of my choice of vocation that no expense was too great for 'God's chosen one'. At the time studying for the priesthood was seen as an entry not only to the kingdom of God, but also to the kingdom of the world.

The Catholic Church in Ireland reigned supreme in each and every aspect of life. Bishops were treated like feudal lords and priests, nuns, and religious brothers like minor royalty. While in some sense I knew this to be true, it was not uppermost in my thoughts in joining the ranks. When I returned from Dublin with my new wardrobe, I had of course to try on my clerical garb for my awe-struck brothers and sisters. They wanted to try on the new blue bathrobe, as no one had ever seen one and thought it both comic and most unusual. It was for people in our neighbourhood. Afterwards, when I would return home on holidays, from seminary, local people would borrow it if they had to go to the hospital.

The new all black suit and clothes that I now wore in my first year of training raised me to a status separate and apart from everyone outside the clerical culture. My parents and grandparents, brothers and sisters would never see me again except through the eyes of 'Mother Church'. I was elated by my newfound state. I did everything I could to cultivate and nourish my vocation. I was totally taken in by the indoctrination, education, and inspiration of those in charge. God's will and the superior's were one, we were told by our Novice Master. Obedience to the bell that would ring for all of our various activities was obedience to the voice of God. We were to have no will of our own. To follow one's own will was seen as listening to the voice of Satan. "Even if I ask you to plant a cabbage upside down, and you know it will not grow, you must obey me as the voice of God," our Master of Novices told us during our first retreat.

My particular friendship or PF as I learned it was called was the first crack in my armour. Jay was my best friend and the boy I first struck up a conversation with when I boarded the train at Ennis railway station. He was just as naive as I was, and looked like a boy who came straight off the farm. For the entire world he was the spit and image of 'John-Boy' from the later T.V. programme 'The Walton's'. Although heterosexual in orientation, for six years we would struggle with our relationship and love.

Jay and I became friends instantly in our first year of training for priesthood. We tried to spend time together and enjoy each other's company as much as possible. In novitiate and later on in seminary, homosexuality—or indeed any kind of sexuality—was never mentioned. Yet it was everywhere. When twenty-six adolescent boys - and later in major seminary one hundred and twenty young men - are thrown together at a time when libidinal hormones are at their most ripe, discouragement from special friendships is demanded. "Nunquam duo, semper tres" – "Never two, always three" - was the motto of all relationships.

Students were not allowed in each other's cubicles at any time of day or night. These cubicles, in a large dormitory, were divided up like horse boxes. Each one had a single bed, a locker, a curtained wardrobe and a wash hand basin with cold water. Over the bed was a large crucifix and each cubicle had a curtain at its entrance to serve as a door. The showers were separate units with doors and bolts in each one, as were the dressing and undressing areas in the sports annex in the major house of studies. At the time I did not question this prudishness. Only much later did I realise how unnatural this arrangement was. On the year of completion of my studies in theology a visiting athletic team made fun of the bolted dressing cubicles, suggesting 'what were we so afraid of . . .?' It was then, for the first time, I realised how artificial our homosocial environment was.

The extraordinary lengths to which the authorities went in order to prevent any threat of sexual arousal in an all male environment, now makes much sense. We know enough from many different sources of research those young men, whether gay or straight, which are thrown together will under certain conditions have sex with each other. In fact, the distinction of sexual orientation seems to become less clear in protracted periods of all male or female environments.

The seminary was such an environment. To my knowledge, homosexual activity was not rife, but did occur between some individuals with some regularity. Most of my contemporaries were so sexually repressed that any kind of sexual expression was totally beyond the pale. On St. Patrick's Day 1965 we were 'allowed' to dance Irish sets with chairs— not each other. Flesh touching flesh even in a dance was forbidden. I was totally taken in by the brainwashing in relationship to my body. On one and only one occasion I was shocked when a fellow novice came up beside me at the urinal and asked: "Can I have a feel?" My sexuality and spirituality for now had landed on different planets.

Jay and I were friends, but were most careful not to stand out from the crowd. Initially we would have no more thought of expressing our friendship physically than we would have thought of having sex with God. We stayed in this hothouse environment without any contact with the outside world for ten whole months. During that time we were not allowed to see family or friends. All the mail we both send and received was opened and read. We were not allowed newspapers, radio or television. Our isolation was as complete as our indoctrination.

At the end of the year, having successfully made our thirty-day retreat and other religious exercises, we were admitted to the pious Society of African Missions. The thirty-day retreat based on the Spiritual Exercises of St Ignatius of Loyola, founder of the Jesuits, was and is a milestone in Catholic spiritual asceticism. It is not suitable for adolescent boys however, and was used in my experience as a way of enforcing the will of those who had charge over us.

Servile obedience was the litmus test of all virtue both at home and in school. This was a big part of the problem when as children and students we were physically and sexually abused. The parent, teacher, priest, and garda had power like the 'Divine Right of Kings'. Any questioning of any authority led to further abuse. The received wisdom was that those in authority knew best and did best. There was no room whatsoever for fallibility. Everyone in authority was infallible. Therefore if one came home to one's parents and said that the teacher was very strict and used the cane a lot, it was assumed by the parents that this was deserved. The mere suggestion to a parent or guardian that a nun, Christian Brother, priest or teacher would touch a student sexually was usually met by sheer and utter denial. It was simply not considered a possibility.

The class division of society at the time was also strictly observed. On top were the clergy, followed by doctors, teachers, and garda. These class distinctions carried on into the classroom. Boys or girls who had fathers or family in these professions or were business people of the town were given special privilege by the nuns and Christian brothers. Those of us from the wrong side of the tracks were exposed to much more hardship and 'kept in our place' by such exercises as being forced to pick up garbage after the more privileged children at lunchtime. Some nuns and brothers with vows of poverty had an extraordinary way of exemplifying their commitment to the poor by boldly courting the rich. I shall always remember during my First Holy Communion celebrations how the nun in charge invited the doctors' wives into the convent out of a shower of rain while the rest of our mothers were left in the convent garden to be soaked on from on high. Such was the given hierarchy of God's favour at the time.

Novitiate and seminary echoed the same system of blind obedience and hierarchical rank and privilege. Although there never was to my knowledge physical or sexual abuse of any kind, the intellectual and psychological subservience required did serious emotional damage to our maturation as human beings. Every single minute of our lives was regulated from dawn to dusk. Individual responsibility was reduced to a minimum, especially during the first years of training. We arose at six in the morning. We had to be in chapel for prayer at six twenty five. This was followed by meditation, Holy Mass and thanksgiving. Then we had housework. The junior students, known as philosophers, were required to clean the toilets of the senior students. These were called the theologians. Then we had breakfast after which we were allowed to break the solemn silence for the first time which had reigned since the night before. This was followed by recreation and classes in philosophy and theology until prayers at twelve forty five.

This particular form of prayer was called the Particular Examine. It was a time to concentrate on a particular virtue that one needed to cultivate or vice to be mastered. I concentrated on Humility as my most important virtue to be cultivated. After lunch, we had manual labour or sporting activities depending on the weather. Four o'clock tea was followed by spiritual reading, rosary, and Vespers. After supper and a short recreation, there was study for two hours and Compline Prayer followed by bed. The idea of questioning any of this regimentation was unthinkable and likely to lead to one's dismissal from the college. In many ways, it was a blissfully happy time as we remained perennial adolescents. There was no responsibility other than to follow the rule. The possibility for abuse and dehumanisation by those in authority and those obeying in such an environment has bloodied pages of history. Luckily for us in seminary at the time, we had men in charge who were people of integrity and true holiness. Men who themselves had been formed or malformed as the case maybe by the same system of blind obedience.

Our studies, while interesting and excellently taught in some cases, depending on the particular professor, did not prepare us for the real world of work and relationship. Only after Ordination did we get any real sense of what life, love, sex, money, and struggle was all about. There was virtually no education around sexuality and sexual emotional maturity. This entire area was relegated to the bin of denial and repression. I left seminary at the age of twenty-five as ignorant about sexuality as when I entered at age seventeen. My growth in this area had been completely stultified. The physiology of a woman's and man's body was completely foreign to me, even though I had the equivalent of a postgraduate education in philosophy and theology.

One of the primary examples of psychosexual arrested development was the fact that the only mortal sin ever committed by most seminarians was masturbation. We knew this because before Mass and the reception of Holy Communion, these students had to confess. Everyone who had masturbated the night before was seen outside the confessional in a public church, waiting to be absolved from "self polluting," as masturbation was called, by one of our professors. This provided much commentary with some hilarity amongst the most voyeuristic in our midst.

I absolutely believed then that masturbation was the only form of sexual activity possible between men. Intercourse between a man and woman for the procreation of children was, I believed, the only other possible sexual activity. The idea of oral sex and anal sex never even occurred to me. My best friend got "so tired of wanking," that he left seminary, "to find a hole to put this in." It never dawned on either of us that with a little spice and imagination, there was so much more sexual activity to be wonderfully enjoyed.

Journal Entry Number 5

One of the primary difficulties in working through the psycho-sexual damage done to people by the Church or other such institutions is the internalised and unconscious deep wounds people carry. All of us who have come through such systems of oppression are at best, as Henri Nouwen put it so well, "wounded healers." As is often the case with a persecuted and long disenfranchised minority the oppression internalised can be turned on other minorities who are struggling themselves for justice and some equal place at the common table of humanity. This is most often the case with racial or ethnic oppression. There are countless examples of racially oppressed peoples turning themselves oppressive toward other races as soon as they get their freedom.

The beloved can become the beloved enemy. The projection of one's own hurt onto people who are totally innocent is probably one of the most painful and distressing pathologies I have experienced when trying to help people overcome their own self-hatred. I don't believe that we are ever healed from all that we have come through. Yet we can learn to live with it and learn how not to allow our hatreds determine how we live and how we love. The following homily was given as an attempt to help raise consciousness around our own hurt. All of us reach a stage in life when everything has to be forgiven.

Homily on Mark 1:29-39

This Gospel reading gives us stories of Jesus healing people. If I had been present, I would have asked the Lord to heal me of my internalised homophobia and psychosexual sickness. More significantly, I would have begged God in Christ to increase my faith in Him, in others, in myself.

Forgive Yourself

Many of us here, out of a lack of proper self-love, have made misjudgements and put the wrong foot forward. As St Bernard of Clairvaux put it, "the most difficult and mature virtue to attain is a mature love of self for God." Like Flannery O'Connor's reflection, "Human nature is so faulty that it can resist any amount of grace and most of the time it does." Even the most blessed among us, if honest, will have had thoughts, words and actions to regret. Most people have made, at some time or another, lamentable and reprehensible choices.

If we can bring ourselves to forgive ourselves – and we should repent and forgive ourselves for any guilt that is rightfully ours – we will come to understand what it is to forgive another. "Forgive as you have been forgiven," that is the golden standard. It applies to all of us as forgivers in need of forgiveness. In order for true Christ-like healing to happen, it is important for us to be grounded in an honest sense of our own guilt over against what is the appropriate guilt of others who have sinned against us. Having separated what is my own sin from how I have been sinned against is necessary in order to move forward in holiness, wholeness, and emotional maturity.

The guilt, the sexual shame, the loss of dignity that belongs to the institutional Church in our regard is thrust into our souls as lesbian, gay, bisexual and transgendered children – and not just us, straight people suffer this abuse – as innocent victims. This venom poisons the soul, sometimes even to death, as was my experience often with gay men dying of HIV/AIDS. The cancer of this 'holy' homophobia has to be exorcised because it is foreign, false, and cannot be incorporated into the true self, which as Thomas Merton reminds us is the God-self.

The self-distortion that results from abusive Church teachings is almost unbearable for some. The burden becomes incomprehensible when an institution that calls itself the Body of Christ heaps opprobrium on those in society who are often most despised and rejected. 'Coming out' is something the Church should be enabling and ennobling, especially for the young. Jesus never softened his condemnation of anyone who would "scandalise one of those little ones."

Yet, as Jesus reminds us, forgiveness is all, forgiveness is everything. He exemplifies this for us every time we come together to celebrate the Eucharist: "On the night he was betrayed, he took bread, blessed it, broke it and gave it to them saying, THIS IS MY BODY." On the night, he was betrayed, mind you.

Forgive Life

Life is not fair or just. Physical, intellectual, emotional, environ-mental, and even spiritual gifts and limitations are bestowed with a mysterious haphazardness. Life endows more of its benefits on some for no special reason. Fate dispossesses others of advantages with an equal caprice. Some of us grow up in homes, neighbourhoods, and circumstances that are nourishing and supportive. Others have endured unspeakable hardship and neglect. Some of us enjoy good health; others are afflicted with pain, suffering and loss. Life gives each of us some good things and deprives us of others.

We cannot control these endowments or events. We do not choose our mooring posts. The path chooses us. Life is what it is. No one can choose her or his inheritance. Nevertheless, we can modify life's endowments, enhance the gifts, and temper the effects of life's limitations. To do so we have to accept life and give up our resistance to reality. Forgive life! Accept life! Acceptance of life – forgiveness of life – gives us freedom to live. To accept life is to accept the God of Life, Love and Freedom.

Summer

Manual work, although encouraged and mandated in seminary, was frowned on when undertaken for monetary gain, especially outside Ireland. Many students such as Jay and I were often broke and needed some pocket money to keep us afloat throughout the academic year. I had little choice but to work at one thing or another to keep myself in cash, not simply with pocket money but more importantly to buy essential books and clothing.

Having secured a job in Pilkington's Glass Factory near Sheffield in England, Jay and I headed off to earn 'our fortune' the first summer we were out of seminary. Sasana, as England was known, had rejected the true faith and become as pagan as deepest Africa according to the Christian Brothers. Protestant England was the same thing as being damned.

We had two Protestant boys in our primary school. They were treated more or less like the rest of us except when it came to catechism classes. Either they had to leave, which marked them out as descendants of Cain, or they were forced to stay and suffer an indoctrination that was both insult and injury to their own faith. This was a time when to darken the door of a Protestant church was considered a mortal sin and necessitated confessing to a priest at the next available opportunity. Arriving in 'Protestant Godless England' was a real revelation to Jay and me. Our fellow workers at the glass factory were highly amused at the seriousness of our vocation at nineteen years of age. They did not make fun of us, but even then we could tell that the whole idea was way beyond them and sounded somewhat barmy. It never occurred to us that we were anything but normal and, of course, with an edge on godliness as we thought, no one other than a Catholic could appreciate our lifestyle.

We were obligated to attend Mass—daily if possible. This proved completely impractical, since we were both on shift

47

work. We did attend whenever our working schedule allowed. It may have been God's revenge on our triumphalism, but we discovered toward the end of our working holiday that the church we had been attending for Mass was in fact High Anglican! Yet, it came complete with Mass in Latin and all the Roman Catholic trimmings, including a picture of the Pope in the vestry of the Church. Jay and I had no idea that such a strand even existed in the Anglican Communion. Our ignorance was such that we thought all Protestants were the same and their worship had nothing like our Mass. On realising that we were attending what was considered a heretical Mass, we had, of course, to go to confession. It was here we met our Waterloo! During the course of the confession, I had to reveal to the priest that I was a clerical student studying in Ireland for the priesthood. I told him I was here in England working for the summer holidays with my fellow student Jay. As usual, the priest questioned me about my sexual life.

One thing followed another, and eventually I found myself confessing that yes, 'sometimes we have sex together.' Attending an Anglican Mass paled into insignificance, and I was told in no uncertain terms that I was not fit to be a priest, indulging as I did in "the unnatural sexual practice of masturbating" . . . One would have thought we had committed murder every time we did so.

The priest threatened to withhold absolution completely. He considered the sin of mutual masturbation as a most serious evil. Withholding absolution from a penitent meant exclusion from Holy Communion. This meant that in seminary I would be shamed as a public sinner. I broke down in tears. The priest on realising my distress eventually gave me absolution on the condition that I would bring the matter of my sexual relationship with Jay into the public forum. In other words I had to tell a priest on the seminary staff the sexual nature of my relationship to Jay. Although I did not realise it at the time, this was a breach of the confessional seal. Yet I was so afraid of being publicly labelled a 'wanker,' and worse still not being allowed to receive Holy Communion, that I would have done anything the confessor asked to get out of the situation in which I found myself.

On my return to seminary, I waited for a while and eventually sought out the priest who would change my life forever. Father Jeremy had arrived at the seminary two years previously. He was less than ten years older than the oldest seminarian. What he lacked in years, he made up for in brilliance of intellect and freedom of expression. No matter the subject, he had a command of language that was inspiring and could communicate his ideas with great lucidity and skill. Consequently, he was looked up to by the student body at large.

Although Jeremy was not one of my professors at the time as I was too young, it was natural to seek out such a popular and young person. I was duty bound to honour the promise I had made to the priest confessor while working in England.

Father Jeremy received me most graciously in his room, and although sympathetic to my predicament, told me that I would have to leave the seminary. Such behaviour was, to his mind, not consonant with my future as a celibate priest. Seminary rules left no room for exceptions. I was devastated. This was and is standard practice in most seminaries. All of my dreams of priesthood, of serving God in the poor, were thrown out the window in one fell swoop.

I returned to my room and cried my eyes out. Eventually I found the courage to tell my friend and sexual partner what happened. He called me 'a bloody eejet' for telling anybody and so putting us both in the dilemma in which we now found ourselves. Subsequently, Jay was summoned to Father Jeremy's room and told that he also would have to leave seminary as there was no room in priesthood for "anyone with these tendencies."

Both Jay and I spent the following days wondering when the shoe on the other foot would drop. How would we tell our parents and families that we both had decided to leave African Missions College? We waited anxiously to be summoned to Father Jeremy's room to be given our days of dismissal. Father Jeremy would first have to bring our situation into the public forum of the seminary council. This forum met at regular intervals to discuss the progress of students in general and their suitability as candidates for Ordination to priesthood in particular.

We knew that as soon as anyone was found out to be homosexually or heterosexually active in any way, then this was considered proof positive that the person had no vocation to celibacy and therefore no vocation to priesthood. As we waited and waited for what seemed like a lifetime, we were assured by Father Jeremy that we would be asked to leave separately so that no one would suspect the reason for our departure. This struck me as somewhat naive, since everyone knew we were best friends and immediately would suspect that our departure three weeks apart was linked for one reason or another.

Eventually, I was summoned to Father Jeremy's room about a week or so after the first disclosure. Jeremy told me to be seated while he reiterated the seriousness and sinfulness of our actions. He asked me to describe in more detail what we had done. I told him that our sexual acting out was essentially mutual masturbation. When he asked, "Have you ever entered each other from behind?" I replied, "O no Father, we always come in the side door." He blushed . . .

What I did not know and would not know until years later Father Jeremy was himself gay and was head over heels in love with me. After a while, the tone of the conversation changed. Father Jeremy informed me that on prayer and reflection he had decided not to bring "our problem" into the public forum and decided to give us a second chance, provided we promised to give up the activity in question. The sigh of relief that I gave on hearing these words was palpable. I was ready to promise the moon and could barely contain myself as I skipped down the corridor to tell Jay the good news. Jay followed suit to Father Jeremy's room and so began our try at celibate friendship.

Journal Entry Number 6

Gay priests, as is well reported and documented, constitute forty to fifty percent of Catholic clergy. (See, for example, *The Changing Face of Priesthood* by Donald B. Cozzens, Minnesota, The Liturgical Press, 2000.)

This is not unique. Women and men of a different sexual orientation have throughout history peopled leadership roles in the arena of the Sacred. (See *Gay American History* by Jonathan Katz, New York, Thomas Y. Crowell Co., 1976.) The Berdache and Shamans of Native Americans immediately come to mind.

Catholic gay priests - and others - continue to occupy this sacred space. Unlike their predecessors in history, priests who are gay – whether celibate or not – are forced to lie about who they are and engage in the most damaging and dangerous psycho-sexual splitting for the sake of the Church. The following is a response to a priest friend - Father Raoul Bunoit - and by extension to his partner who like so many priests straight and gay fall in love.

The Church mandates celibacy for all priests. The choice is to give up priesthood or the partner you love. Heterosexual priests can seek laicisation and be married in Church. Gay priests cannot. All gay priests – and all unmarried Catholics - who live in love, live in sin according to Church teaching. Father Bunoit, unlike so many of his fellow priests, had both the courage and integrity 'to do the right thing' by the man he loved.

Dear Raoul,

I don't envy you your situation. I feel at a very deep level 'it could have been my own' some twenty years ago . . . I want to tell you to 'let go, turn over a new leaf and start over.' I wish I could even do it for you as a friend. But alas, asking you to move on 'without priesthood' is as impossible as I doing it for you . . .

The fact is you have to live with and without the priesthood. The institutional recognition of priesthood is denied you because of who you are and how you love. Wear that badge as an honour . . . *how you love* . . . Yet living within it can be so very difficult. It demands a wholeness and holiness that is gift, grace, and painful acceptance.

This ineluctable hunger for priesthood and love enfleshed in another man will often leave you feeling both in this world and not of it, or of this world but not in it. It is a dangerous place, because I believe it is the crossroads between heaven and hell. As you well know, it is so easy to miss the signs and choose a stone for bread. Priests who are sexually oriented toward their own gender struggle with these both within and outside the institution.

You have chosen to be an 'inside outsider' and have not yet found 'a job' that you like. Consequently, your depression/ pain is much more acute and accentuated. Even if you did find the perfect job/priesthood I believe that because you belong to an institution that does spiritual violence to gay people – to *you* – you will, like our brother priests, find you are always in a certain sense homeless. The place of your spiritual-cultural nurturing says you are 'deformed' and cannot love what your heart desires. The wreckage of this abominable teaching lies strewn across the Catholic world in the lives of LGBT people. Even the best of our leaders and 'heroes' are deeply wounded. The Catholic Church does not accept gay love. That is poison to the soul.

You already know all this. We have often talked about it. But sometimes we need to be reminded by those who love us, as to how in fact this 'toxic grace' affects our own psyche and soul. What do you do is again and again the question. The simple answer is, I don't know. I have never really known: that is the truthful answer, even when all appearances were to the contrary.

I believe, as I said at the beginning of this letter, that with grace you 'learn to live with it'. Practically speaking, you find a way – with some meaning – of bringing in some income. You learn to live in this world of shadows, feeling your way as best you can. Sometimes you barely get enough light to take the next step. Yet you are only expected to take that step for which light has been given. Do that for now. It is enough, my friend.

With love always.

Bernárd.

Late Summer

Jay eventually decided that the clerical life was not for him and so ten months prior to ordination he took the very courageous step of leaving the seminary. I was of course broken-hearted. I remember this day as if it were yesterday. In no way could I share with anyone the pain and emptiness that I was feeling. I would have been laughed out of court. The day he left, I avoided people as much as I could and took to the hills for a long cross country run. As Kierkegaard would say, "love is in the absence." I did not realise how much I was in love with Jay until he left. Eventually he found a good woman to love and with whom to have a family. We have remained close friends to this very day.

After Jay's departure, celibacy took on a new poignancy. I believed that now that the temptation to have physical congress with Jay was removed, I would naturally and necessarily settle into the chaste life demanded of me by my upcoming Ordination to the Diaconate. This is the final stage before Ordination to priesthood itself. In my case and those of my contemporaries, it was conferred six months prior to our Ordination to priesthood. The ceremony presided over by the local bishop involved taking a vow of celibacy and an oath to remain permanently in the Society of African Missions.

The vow of celibacy, while encapsulating the chastity incumbent on all Catholics, also forbids marriage for life. It is worthy of note that at this particular juncture of Church history, after Vatican Council II in the early 1960s there was a great air of optimism that this rule of celibacy would be removed. After all, we argued the rule was man-made and most of Jesus' Apostles, the first priests, were married. We were in the throes of the renewal of Vatican II, and everything from church language and liturgy was in the process of change. The four of us being ordained subsequently refused to have the words 'A Priest Forever' printed on the cover of our ordination booklet. 'A Priest' yes. 'Forever' celibate no.

The lead-up to Ordination to priesthood was as exciting and awe-inspiring as a child's anticipation of Santa Claus at Christmastime. Here was the culmination of a life-dream. This is what had filled my head and heart ever since my boyhood days when I would put on my mother's dress and play saying Mass with Marietta biscuits and water. Now at last my true self would be realised and recognised for what it was and what God had created it to be.

The days preceding the big day were spent on retreat in prayer at the Redemptorist monastery in Clonnard, Belfast. At this time in Northern Ireland, 'the Troubles' were predominant in everyone's mind. Clonnard monastery in the heart of Belfast was a sanctuary for many a troubled Catholic. There was a heavy British army presence in the area and the atmosphere was tense. Apart from 'periodic visits' by the British army to Dromantine College, our lives in seminary were generally uninterrupted by the tragedy that was unfolding around us.

After the retreat, I returned to the seminary to meet my parents, family, and friends who had travelled North of the border to join me on this most auspicious occasion. No expense had been spared to mark this great day. Everyone had new outfits and was in high spirits. My father and mother were as proud as punch and my sisters and brothers gave the impression that they were about to be inaugurated into Burke's Peerage.

While overjoyed at the upcoming realisation of my boyhood dreams of being a priest, I carried a deep loneliness that nothing or no one could overcome. I was delighted to be the centre of attention, but there was a vast deep sadness in me that would gnaw at my very soul even during the most sacred Ordination ceremony itself. I had a secret that I had no words to express, or even if I had the words there was no one with whom I dared share them.

This 'sinful-sickness' that I experienced at the very depth of my being would remain closeted and alienated for some time to come. Jay was generously present at my Ordination and was the master of ceremonies at my reception the following day in the Queens Hotel in Ennis. He knew what troubled me, but in the deeply homophobic Ireland of the 1960s and 1970s—when homosexual love was still a crime—he prayed with me that with time and grace these thoughts and feelings would disappear.

My first Mass in the pro-Cathedral of Ennis town was an extraordinary event. The Christian Brothers' School Choir led the singing. The entire school attended the Mass, together with my younger sisters' classes from the Convent of Mercy primary school. The chairman of the local urban council—together with my parents, maternal grandparents, sisters and brothers, uncles and aunts from both sides of the family, cousins, neighbours and friends—all gathered to celebrate with the newly ordained priest and receive a first blessing.

The joyful atmosphere in the church was palpable. I had never seen my parents prouder or happier. My father and sister Mary read the lessons, and my youngest brother Patrick served at the altar together with my cousin Pádraig from Cork. As people lined up afterwards to be blessed and to kiss my newly consecrated hands, I guess I felt like some kind of pop star, totally overwhelmed by the adulation and isolation of it all.

No amount of public adulation could force the pain in me to be God. During the next month, I went around my hometown visiting and blessing everyone. It was an exhausting schedule. People then – and maybe now – expected so much of their priests. I suddenly became the recipient of all kinds of confidences and secrets. People spoke openly about their troubled marriages and relationships, their hopes and joys as well as their fears and their doubts. While I always considered myself a good and compassionate listener, I was ill prepared for the deluge that flooded my young priestly ears. I was relieved to return to seminary at the end of January to complete my studies and bask for the last time in the comfort of answers that had no questions.

On return, we were faced with what has become known as one of the greatest travesties of justice in the entire history of Northern Irish politics. Bloody Sunday 30 January 1972 in the Bogside of Derry city awakened in the 'silent Catholic majority' unprecedented outrage against the murder of young defenceless Nationalists by the British army.

This was the first and only time the seminary Superiors and staff, together with the entire student body, got involved in the politics of the North. We marched – although forbidden by law – in Newry to protest against the killings. I was both stunned and awed by the presence of thousands upon thousands of people, together with hundreds of nuns, religious brothers, and priests in their habits marching silently and with great dignity, as army helicopters flew over our heads blasting through loudspeakers: "You are breaking the law, disband immediately."

This was my first taste of civil disobedience. There was more to come. Seminary students from the Falls Road Nationalist area of Belfast had told 'us Southerners' – students from the Irish Republic - that we had no idea of the discrimination most Catholics suffered at the hands of the Protestant majority. We hadn't . . .

In the ninety-five percent Catholic Republic, most of us were abysmally ignorant of the 'apartheid' system on our doorstep. This changed forever in 1969 when civil unrest combined with decades of mounting frustration and anger spilt onto the streets of Northern Ireland. I saw how bitterly some Catholics and Protestants hated each other, even though as individuals whom I knew on both sides, they seemed very likeable. I was forced to stretch my thinking to realise that sincere and honest people could believe in very divergent political and religious doctrines.

In profound ways, I for the first time emancipated myself from Catholic triumphalism and became deeply committed to the ecumenical movement. This independence of thought caused great pain and stress to many of my peers, but looking back on it, it was when I became an independent person. Of course there was much revolt and rebellion in my attitude during that period, but the essential growth was achieved which has permeated both my attitude and behaviour toward Christianity ever since.

Journal Entry Number 7

Christianity and Prejudice

Nothing in the study of religions requires that they cross the line of our acceptance in a photo finish. Yet, perhaps we are able to see them more as faiths of real people who are asking the same basic questions that we are—seekers like us of the illumined life.

In the midst of all religions, there stands no one so incomparably superior that no significant truth is to be found in one that is not present in equal or clearer form in another. Does not each contain some version of the Golden Rule? If all truth essential to 'life with God' can be found in one religion, can it not also be found in different and diverse ways in others? If God is a God of Love, it seems most unlikely that He or She would be so selective in the choice of one group over another? It seems equally probable that such a God would take different facets and different forms according to the differences in nature of different souls and the differences in character of local traditions and civilizations. This is one possible contemporary meaning of Saint Paul's statement, "one spirit, and many gifts". One who holds this view will find many things in other religions that puzzle and disturb, but will see their own light as deriving basically from the same Source.

Over twenty-five hundred years ago, it took an exceptional man like Socrates to say on his deathbed, "I am not an Athenian or a Greek but a citizen of the world." Today I believe we must all struggle towards these words. We have come to the point in history when anyone who is 'only Irish, English or American, Jewish, Christian or Muslim' is not all they can be. The other part of one's being which beats with the pulse of all humanity has yet to be born.

To borrow Nietzsche's image, we all have been summoned to

become Cosmic Dancers who do not rest heavily on a single spot
but lightly turn and leap from one position to another. We shall
all have our own perspectives, but they can no longer be cast in
the hard moles of oblivion to the rest. The Cosmic Dancer, the
World Citizen, will be an authentic child of his parent culture but
related closely to all. Such a person or people will not identify
their whole being with any one land, however dear. They may
pride themselves in their culture or nationality, but this will be
an affirming pride born of gratitude from values gained, not a
defensive pride whose only device for achieving the sense of
superiority it pathetically needs is by grinding down others
through invidious comparison. Their roots in family, community,
and their civilization will be deep, but in that very depth they
will strike the water table of common humanity, and thus
nourished will reach out in more active curiosity, more open
vision, to discover and understand what others have seen. For is
the other not also human? If only we might see what has interested others, might it not interest us as well? It is an exciting
prospect. The classic ruts between native and foreign, barbarian
and Greek, East and West, will be softened if not effaced. Instead
of crude and boastful contrasts, there will be borrowings and
exchange, mutual help, cross-fertilization that leads sometimes
to good strong hybrids but for the most part simply enriches the
species in question and continues its vigour.

The practical gains that come from being able to look at the
world through the eyes of another people are enormous. They
can enable industry to do business with China; they can keep a
nation from tripping up so often in a crowded and busy world.
Yet, the greatest gains need no tally. To glimpse what belonging
means to a Vietnamese; to sense with a Burmese grandmother
what passes in life and what endures; to understand how a
Hindu can understand his personality as only a mask overlaying
and obscuring the Infinite beneath and see how he can accept
personal and impersonal views of God as equally true; to crack

the paradox of a Zen monk who will assure you there is no difference in thieving and charity but who would never dream of thieving himself – to swing such things into view is to introduce a whole new dimension into the glance of Spirit. It is to have another world to live in. The only good without qualification is not as Immanuel Kant argued the good will – a will can mean well within terribly narrow confines. The only good without qualification is extended vision, the enlargement of one's understanding and awareness of what reality is ultimately like.

The surest way to the heart of a people is through their religion, assuming that it is still alive and has not been fossilized. Wherever religion comes to life, it displays a startling quality; it takes over. All else, while not silenced, becomes subdued and thrown without contest into a supporting role. Religion alive confronts the individual with the most momentous option this world can present. It calls the soul to the highest adventure it can undertake, a proposed journey across the jungles, peaks, and deserts of the human spirit. The call is to confront reality, to master the self. Those who dare to hear and follow this secret call soon learn the dangers and difficulties of its lonely journey.

The sharp edge of a razor is difficult to pass over;
Thus the wise say the path to Salvation is hard.
Katha-Upanishad

Certainly such a profound endeavour is not reconcilable with prejudice of any kind.

Summer Ends

If the taste of priesthood was a little daunting after Ordination, then my arrival in Zambia, Central Africa, on my first missionary assignment was overwhelming.

Nothing had prepared me for the culture shock that ensued. I had never in my life seen so many black people. At first, I confess I could not distinguish one from another. Growing up I met only one black person who was doing his internship at the local hospital in Ennis. He was referred to as Saint Martin. The only image of black people we had was that of St Martin de Porres, a popular Peruvian saint to whom we prayed when sick. In fact one of my neighbours on coming out of an anaesthetic after an operation exclaimed, "O my God I've died and gone to heaven," on seeing the black intern for the first time at the foot of her bed. As I tried to settle in and acclimatise, I could distinguish people one from the other. I also interestingly began to see facial and physical resemblances to people I knew back home.

For three months, I was sent to language school in Illondola in the north of the country. Here a group of French missionaries, the White Fathers, had set up a school to teach the language, customs, and culture of the native people. Having completed the course, I was sent to work as assistant priest in the parishes of Kabushi and Ndeke.

The parish of Kabushi had a somewhat solid structure for a church, with a parish hall attached. The parish of Ndeke consisted of a huge shanty town with thousands of people living in what can only be described as appalling conditions. The so-called houses were made of corrugated iron, cardboard, and wood thrown together in whatever way would best give protection from the elements. There were mud floors and open sewers with garbage and vermin everywhere. Our church consisted of a galvanised structure on a mud floor. The altar was an orange crate draped in a white cloth with a beer mug as a holy water font.

The people themselves were amazingly resilient and extremely friendly. They lived from hand to mouth and took their faith very seriously. They loved the liturgy of the Catholic Mass and would spend hours singing and praying to their hearts' content. I was both in awe of them and deeply disturbed by the terrible poverty.

Although, I did not come from an affluent background, seeing children with bloated stomachs from hunger was beyond my wildest imaginings. With time, the Church helped build schools and get better housing with sanitation. The priests and nuns with whom I worked there were inspirational in their devotion to Christ and dedication to the poor. To this day, when I despair of institutional Catholicism, I think of these women and men. Their presence is a shining light as beautiful as God.

One of the inroads I made while working there was to have a drama group of students perform in the Lowenthal Theatre in Ndola. This until now was an all white enclave. Through some contacts I had made with English friends working in the copper mines, we were able to stage the first all black African cast in an enjoyable theatrical performance. Last year, I had an unexpected contact from one of the young men who performed in this play. He 'heard I was gay' and wanted to know was I 'ok?' He reminded me of how important this first drama was for them. He now lives and teaches in London. I was delighted to meet with this man after almost forty years, and grateful to hear his compassionate concern in my regard.

Despite the tremendous challenge and great demand for humanitarian work, I was not happy there. I was terribly lonely. I could not find a soul mate and missed Jay more than I could say. I tried—God did I try—to find a confidant with whom I could discuss my situation. There was no one who had either the skill or knowledge necessary to empathise or help.

Everything was sin and un-natural. The very thought of been

told this again and again drove me more in on myself. I used to drive to Ndola airport at night and sit in the mission car facing toward London watching the planes take off. I would watch with longing for someone to speak to. I was confused as to who I was and what I was feeling. I did know that inside of me, I was not the same as the others and felt agonisingly tortured that I could not find decent words to say what I felt. The fact that a beautiful young and deeply committed nun had a crush on me only compounded the matter. I knew how this woman felt for me, but I could not reciprocate. All the while, I thought I would eventually get the grace to be like the rest of men—normal!

After much contemplation and prayer, I decided I had to find some kind of exit from the inner hell I was living. My superiors did not take kindly to my request. Although I had been on the missions for two years, I was not due leave for another twelve months. After some heated discussion, I was allowed to return to Ireland for a break. There was no specific reason other than that I was extremely unhappy. Although thoughts of suicide did cross my mind, some kind of hope still flickered within me.

The African Missions Society, as with all Church institutions, was primarily interested in keeping the show on the road. To have a young priest such as me break ranks was very much frowned on. Consequently, my welcome at the headquarters in Cork city was a muted affair. Lucky for me, I found one of our priests who had trained as a counsellor and was able to hear and help make some sense of my pain. He suggested to the Provincial that I be sent for further studies in psychological counselling to Boston University. While there, I would seek the help I needed to sort myself out. Father Jeremy, who was then teaching in London, added his powerful voice to my plea for help in realising this opportunity.

In August of 1975, I arrived in New York City. The Archdiocese of New York was looking for priests to assist in their parishes. They had written to my Superior with the request for priests assigned to further studies. The diocese would supply food, accommodation, and a small stipend to such priests leaving them sufficient time to pursue their academic goals. Consequently, my pursuit of a degree in counselling was switched from Boston College to Fordham University, New York. Here was a culture shock of a completely different kind.

I had first been to New York in 1969 on a student exchange programme. During my seminary years, as already stated, I had to work most summers in order to clothe myself, pay for my text books, and have pocket money. In 1969, with Ordination to priesthood only eighteen months away, I was acutely aware of the burden of expense that this great occasion would place on my parents. The realisation of this fact propelled me to seek more lucrative employment in 'the land of the free and home of the brave'. Subsequently, through a fellow clerical student, I received employment as a waiter in Leeds, Greene County, in upstate New York. This was and still is a very picturesque holiday village in the Catskill Mountains. Here, in an Irish holiday resort hotel and motel run by a very able and successful Sligo woman and her family, I had my first taste of work in the United States of America.

When I arrived in New York City for my orientation programme at the Hotel Pennsylvania on Seventh Avenue at 33rd Street in June 1969, I did not think that this huge metropolis would one day become the home of my heart. I was flabbergasted by the enormity of the place and multiplicity of cultures and peoples in the city. Although my stay in Manhattan was short-lived, the city and its unforgettable buzz left an indelible mark on my soul.

After a week viewing the sights and getting oriented to the city, I boarded a Greyhound bus at Port Authority to take me to my summer work at the Sligo Hotel and Motel in Green County, New York. I spent three glorious months there, waiting on tables all day and working the bar at night. I was also available for singing on request with whatever band would happen to be in residence for the entertainment of the customers. My singing career took off quite by accident. On the first evening of my arrival, I was invited to give a song 'from the old sod,' seeing that I had just arrived 'off the boat'. From then on, I learnt more Irish songs and ballads within a week than Christy Moore in a month of Sundays. Of course, my efforts were richly rewarded, and I became the popular Irish lad who was studying for the priesthood. I can still hear Irish Americans calling for me to sing 'Boola Boola' because they could not pronounce the name of the song 'Boolavogue'.

During my time there, I had no consciousness about my gay identity in any liberating sense. I still believed that it was sin—a cross that I had to bear. The fact that I showed no interest in any of the beautiful and very attractive young girls working and vacationing in the area did not raise an eyebrow with friends or colleagues. After all, according to local lore and the prevailing Irish American Catholic culture that was the unquestioned inheritance of almost all our customers, 'I was watching my priestly vocation.' This I completely accepted myself and never got involved with dating men or women.

I loved the job and the people for whom I worked. I was in my glory performing and meeting and greeting customers. Our patrons, although not rich, were very comfortable materially and generous with their dollars. There was plenty of good food and drink all around. Everyone I met had his or her own automobile, worked and played hard. Here, unlike the Ireland I grew up in, people were rewarded for hard work. Even a menial job, like pressing buttons on a lift paid well. The person who did this task was called an elevator operator. This title struck me as terribly sophisticated. To my inexperienced ears this sounded more like someone working on the space programme at Cape Canaveral, now called Cape Kennedy. Being a 'student priest', I became 'the white-headed boy' of many and the darling would-be priest of some.

While there, I discovered *Playboy* magazine for the first time and took great pride and dare I say satisfaction in the fact that I could masturbate to its pictures. I really believed that this was a sign from God that my prayers were being answered. I was turning straight at last. After what I can only describe as the most glorious summer of my life, I returned to Ireland laden with gifts for all my family and enough money to pay for my Ordination reception the following year.

Returning to New York six years later with such wonderful memories filled me with joy. I was assigned to a parish in the Northwest Bronx. After my experience in Africa of such poverty, the affluence of rectory living was at once both disturbing and comforting. There was no lack of food here, and our every material need was catered for. We had very little money of our own, but all around us was evidence of 'the American dream.' I signed up for my courses in counselling psychology at Fordham University at Lincoln Center.

My mentor – a rather austere older Jesuit – accepted me for the programme of studies on condition that I achieved a B+ average and went into personal psychoanalysis with a psychiatrist of his recommendation. The academic requirements did not worry me too much. I had already come through seminary and, indeed, since leaving the Christian Brothers in Ennis, found academia to my liking and interest. The brutality of my primary and secondary school education, despite having scarred me for life, did not stymie my intellectual growth.

Going into psychoanalysis was a completely different matter. To my Irish mind, this was analogous to sickness. Only the mentally ill went to psychiatrists. They usually were locked up in high stone-walled institutions. This imprisonment often lasted a lifetime. People in those days were scared of the 'mentally ill' and treated them with a mixture of pity and fear. Surely, I was not one of them? At the same time, I had sought this situation out and knew in the depths of my being that I needed help. I very soon realised that in New York, a person without a therapist, or 'shrink' as we called them, is like an elephant without a trunk. It seemed as if everyone is, has been, or desires to be in therapy. This realisation helped me greatly overcome my initial embarrassment about the matter.

I had two days' duty a week in the parish as well as having to be there on weekends to help out with Masses and confession. I settled in very well and quickly succeeded in making friends with people. As I studied, I began to bring the psychological learning into my homilies and talks during Mass. People were moved and keenly interested by the combination of post-Vatican II theology and psychology. As time went by, I was asked to give a weekly course on psychology and theology in the parish hall. This request came from the parishioners themselves. So, with the approval of the pastor, I started a Monday Night group that is now in existence today, over thirty years later.

Having received a very good grounding in theology, primarily from my priest friend and professor, Father Jeremy, in seminary, I was fascinated with the link between theology and psychology. I intuited that good theology would make good psychology. Consequently, I applied myself with diligence to my studies and read everything I could lay my hands on about the connections between the two disciplines. I flourished and received the necessary grades without much difficulty.

My psychoanalysis was another matter. Here I was digging to the very foundations of my being, and what I was coming up with was anything but a pleasant picture. I had been reared on the teaching 'honour thy father and thy mother'. In fact, it was the commandment of my childhood and bore itself out in all my attitudes and behaviour towards those in authority. Respect for authority and avoidance of sex were the paradigms of my psychological formation both at home and in seminary.

Now, I was finding out for the first time my real feelings

about some of those who exercised authority over me, and it was not a pretty sight. In fact, it bore blood and gore over all my landscape. Nightmares were to follow the likes of which I had never experienced before or since. I was traumatised for the first two years of my analysis.

The realisation of my feelings of lovelessness as a boy frightened me. They sent me spiralling into paroxysms of despair. It is not that I found that I was unloved as a child. On the contrary, my parents like all parents of their generation, loved me for who they believed I was, their straight son. In fact, as I previously mentioned, my parents could not have loved me more. Both my parents had accepted me as gay as soon as I came out to them in 1982. My father had taken the unprecedented and most courageous step of going on national television in a programme made by Channel 4 in 1990 to say that he loved me, as he did all his children, irrespective of our sexual orientation. But my inner world, at a time and place where practically nothing was known about psychosexual difference was one of confused sexual identity. My experience as a child, like practically all LGBT children, was one of not having been loved or wanted as child who was psychosexually different. The feelings were so deep and the despair so dark that I wished that I had been aborted.

This distinction between outer experience and inner experience is very necessary as it avoids the blame game. In that sense, no one is to blame. Most parents on discovering that a daughter or son is lesbian or gay immediately start blaming themselves for what they perceive very often as an abnormality. Again and again I have been asked by parents of gays, "where have I gone wrong?" The facts are no one goes wrong, or is to blame for how God creates in His gay image each child, just as He does all children of heterosexual orientation. We are born that way. Hopefully, with the advancement of knowledge and greater tolerance of difference, parents of future generations will be as open to the possibility of LGBT children, as they are to their straight offspring. This has joyfully been the case of my husband Billy and me in relationship to our siblings, their spouses and their children. Our sisters and brothers have brought up their daughters and sons to treat us and our marriage the same as they do their straight uncles and aunts. This is indeed a great blessing and something for which we both are forever grateful.

Having experienced myself as a boy unloved in the very essence of my maleness (or lack thereof) predisposed me to seek the help that I now desperately needed to accept my god given nature. As yet, in my therapy, I was not at all ready to say I was gay. I was still fighting it and wanting desperately to be 'normal'. Who in their right mind in 1975, I thought, would have wanted to admit—like a confession of sin—that they were indeed sick, sinful, and criminal?

This fight was not to last. In my class at Fordham, I had a best friend called Jimmy. He was a mathematical scholar. I was not. I agreed to help him out with the more philosophical parts of the coursework, if he would help me with the statistical analysis. We became good friends. I had few friends in New York at this time as I was still in the birth pangs of making my home in the city that I would come to love. Jimmy, like me, was in his mid-to-late twenties, still living at home and working on a counselling degree with a view to a career change. After evening class we would often go for a beer together, before taking the subway train to 231st Street in the Bronx. We lived in the same area in next-door parishes. His family was Irish American.

Being an FBI (Foreign Born Irish), as we native Irish were called by the Irish Americans, Jimmy showed great interest in the land of my birth. He had never been to Ireland, but like so many of his ethnicity, he had a great nostalgia for the 'old sod'. It was he who introduced me in many ways to the street smarts of a Bronx, New York City native, for which I was very grateful. Since we had to travel on the subway through Harlem and the South Bronx to get home, he told me never to dress up. "Always dress down," he warned me, "and then you are less likely to be robbed on the train."

This was a time when New York was going through its worst fiscal crisis and the city, and the subway in particular, were not safe places. Times Square and Eighth Avenue, for example, was a haven for drug addicts, pimps, and prostitutes. In fact, Eighth Avenue was known as the Minnesota Strip because so many kids from the Midwest ended up selling themselves on the street there to survive. It was for this reason that Father Bruce Ritter founded Covenant House as a place of refuge and hospitality for runaways in 1972 in New York.

When it came time for me to receive my Master's degree in May 1977, I chose not to attend since graduations were primarily family events. Given that I had no family in New York, I thought it better to have my degree mailed to me and forego the ceremony. I was in my room in the rectory when a call came through from another classmate of mine. Sounding terribly distressed, he told me that he had just heard that my friend Jimmy had thrown himself from Fordham University's 26th floor onto the concrete plaza below—from the very floor where we had attended class as graduate students.

I was completely devastated by this horrific news. I never detected in Jimmy even a hint of such tragic hopelessness and despair. How could I be so blind, I asked myself? Why did I not see something, anything that would have given me a hint of his great unhappiness? Blaming myself for being so stupid and terribly upset at such a waste and loss of life, I telephoned Jimmy's pastor. He suggested that I come to the wake and said that he would introduce me to the family as a fellow student and friend of Jimmy's.

Two days later, I concelebrated Jimmy's funeral Mass in a crowded church, as I fought to hold back tears of pain and the loss of my newfound and dear friend. After the Mass, as we blessed Jimmy's coffin, and it was being taken away for burial, I noticed a small group of young men standing apart as it were from the crowd. Whether through inspiration or mere curiosity, I went over to them and asked them how they knew Jimmy. "Jimmy was gay," a young man named Andy replied, "and we are members of a group called Dignity to which Jimmy belonged." I felt as if I had been kicked in the stomach and found it hard to speak. "Come and celebrate Mass for us sometime," he suggested, before I had time to get away.

Back in the room of my rectory, I could not wait for another session with my analyst. I called him up straight away and asked for an appointment. The session was one long crying-jag of guilt and self-blame. Eventually, with great reticence, I admitted 'that I might have feelings similar to those that killed Jimmy'. This was to be a watershed in my psychoanalysis. Through the meaningless death of my young friend, I struggled toward the light. I eventually found the courage to telephone Dignity and ask where and when they met.

In this first decade after the Stonewall Rebellion of 1969—when LGBT people fought back against police repression and sparked a revolution—gay life was blossoming in New York. Gay bars—nice ones, not dismal Mafia-run dens—were opening up all over the place. There were all kinds of social and support groups springing up for LGBT people who wanted to meet others like themselves.

Also flourishing at this time was a plethora of bath houses and bars with dark backrooms where men could have anonymous sex. This was, after all, the adolescence of the gay community and pre-AIDS. What had been labelled as criminal, sick, and sinful – sexual activity between same-gendered people – was now seen as revolutionary and liberating—a counter blow against oppression and repression. The 'free love' of the 1960s for heterosexuals had finally had erupted into the LGBT communities. Many gay people were like kids in a candy store and the song 'Ain't No Stopping Us Now' summed up the feelings of a whole generation.

I stepped into this arena when I made my first contact with Dignity.

Journal Entry Number 8

Lesbian and gay people until very recently had no models of how to be fully human in an anti-gay world. Everything and everyone militated against our being normal. As I have often said, we are the only minority born of parents who do not know how to love us as their gay children. We usually have to learn, first and foremost, how to love and accept ourselves. This, of course, is a lifelong task for everybody, straight and gay. Then in the ordinary course of events, we have to teach our parents how to love and accept us. With the greater awareness of the existence of gay people, this is becoming easier in certain western democracies. It was not so and is not so for the greater majority of LGTB people worldwide.

When Father John McNeill, S.J. published his ground breaking book, *The Church and the Homosexual* (4th ed., Boston: Beacon Press) in 1976 and came out as a gay man himself, he became an instant hero of iconic stature. At last, a 'normal looking', middle-aged scholar identified himself as being one of us. I wrote this article for the Lesbian and Gay Christian Movement, to mark John McNeill's first and only visit to London in September 2000.

Welcome John McNeill

I was on my way to see my shrink on Fifth Avenue and 66th Street the day John McNeill's book *The Church and the Homosexual* hit the front pages of *The New York Times*. The year was 1976. I don't know if I was looking for a cure for my homosexuality or some kind of immaculate deception to deal with my priestly celibacy and emerging homosexual consciousness. What I do know is that the sight of McNeill's book being reviewed did more for my psychological health than the thousands of dollars and hundreds of hours spent in therapists' offices until then.

Father McNeill's book opened for millions of lesbian and gay Catholics and others worldwide a door to freedom that no amount of oppression could ever close. I was elated as I floated into Doctor Padovano's office. Here at last was hope.

Prior to this, I had read everything that I could lay my hands on in Catholic moral theology regarding homosexuality. The combined effect was a constipation of thought followed by diarrhoea of despair. But now with McNeill's book, here at last was a true work of scholarship, meticulously researched and beautifully executed. Scripturally and theologically, it broke new ground, and for over the next twelve months John McNeill's face was everywhere from network television chat shows to national news magazines.

John was instrumental in founding the New York chapter of Dignity in 1972. His work and experience in those early days (less than three years after Stonewall), with Catholic gay men "compelled" him, he once told me, to respond in whatever way he could to the "loneliness, pain, and anguish" of his gay brothers. Having been attracted early on in his studies to Maurice Blondel, a French pre-existentialist philosopher from the turn of the century, he found his Jesuit vocation summed up in a passage of Blondel's: "One must give all for the all."

Certainly, this created the theoretical basis for his movement into political and social activism. He was a Jesuit for almost forty years before his expulsion in 1987 for his views on lesbian and gay sexuality. He had obediently observed his silencing by the Vatican in 1977. John hoped that his silence would "speak eloquently", together with other greats like Blondel, Teilhard de Chardin, John Courtney Murray, and Henri de Lubac. Yet ten years was not enough for the new homophobic hegemony in Rome. "Forced" to speak in response to the "evil" oppression of Cardinal Ratzinger's letter on *The Pastoral Care of Homosexual People*, Fr McNeill gave up membership of the religious family –

the Jesuits – that he loved as much as life itself.

John met his lifetime companion, Charlie Chiarelli, in 1965 at the Avignon papal palace in France. (I have always wondered which one of them tried on the papal tiara first!) John and Charlie's relationship of love has done as much and possibly more, in bearing witness to the Christ-likeness of homosexual love about which he has spent his life writing and teaching.

By the time he published *Taking a Chance on God* in 1988 the landscape had changed decisively. Now John McNeill was offering another challenge: "If religions were not welcoming to lesbian, gay and transgendered people, why should we be open to them?" Where and to what "is the Holy Spirit calling us as lesbian, gay, bisexual and transgendered people of faith?" How can we receive "our spiritual nourishment from our oppressors?"

With *Freedom, Glorious Freedom* in 1995, the subtitle tells all: 'The Spiritual Journey to the Fullness of Life for Gays, Lesbians, and Everybody Else'. In this book he describes much of what happened to him along the way, especially how his spiritual life was enriched by being gay and vice versa. He does not strike out against those who wronged him, but describes with remarkable equanimity and charity how the same Jesuit 'discernment of spirits' brought him to coming out and speaking out. The congruence of his position on the need to live with integrity between both truth and appearance propelled John McNeill to a mature, healthy self-acceptance, and an equally mature, healthy insistence that the rest of us and the Church do the same. It is this message that he shares with clients and audiences, this congruency between what you see and what you get that makes him who he is.

As the inspirational feminist theologian Mary Hunt has so often said: "What John has become is an honest man in love, in sharp contrast to so many of his fellow priests who love with fear or who just fear. He does not need to hide Charlie, pretend that he is celibate, nor choose between ministry and marriage. He has it all, and he deserves it. John did for Catholicism what the Stonewall revolution did for the gay world; he fought back against those who would discriminate. His great work earned him the opprobrium of Rome, but it also put the rest of us in his debt, as he pioneered a struggle that by all Christian values ought to be long over by now, yet sadly still needs to be fought."

He says that his tombstone will read 'Here lays a gay priest who took a chance on God!' Cynics among us would probably have given up on God, Jesus, the Church, and the Jesuits long ago had we not experienced John. He is, indeed, as we say in the Irish language, 'Duine le Dia.' A man with God. A true hero . . .

Welcome John and Charlie. It is good for us that you are here.

Early Autumn

Without knowing, I had already ventured into a gay bar in Greenwich Village, while taking a day tour of lower Manhattan. I found out that it was a gay bar, when I mentioned casually at dinner in the rectory, that I had been sightseeing in the Village. Afterwards, the associate pastor took 'this greenhorn aside,' and explained that there were certain parts of the city, especially certain bars, that were no-go areas for young clerics. They were "full of faggots, queers, and homosexuals." I was left in no doubt that such people were beyond the pale and not to be associated with in any way. (The assistant pastor who told me this I accidentally found in bed with a fellow priest from the parish next door one year later.)

Although desperate at one level to make contact with people like me, it took all my courage to call the Dignity contact number. While my psychiatrist was supportive of my efforts, with two hourly sessions a week, this was but a chink in my armour of self-hating oppression and denial. I was scared out of my cotton-pickin' mind to admit that I might be 'one of them'. How could I ever be one *of them?* After all, I was first and foremost a priest and therefore my sexuality could not and would not define me — especially a dirty, distorted, perverted, sick, and sinful version of sexuality. I was not unnatural, as I had been taught all homosexuals were all of my life.

When I arrived at the Church of the Good Shepherd near Lincoln Center on the West Side of Manhattan, I was shocked to discover that it was a Protestant and not a Catholic Church. The venue fitted my ignorance and prejudice. It fed further my self-loathing – as if it needed such feeding. I inwardly believed that no decent church would accept us.

The first evening I went there, I cowered into the back row of seats. I gave a false name and profession when asked who I was and what I did for a living. This internalised homophobia is of course the greatest weapon the Church and society has against the freedom and dignity of LGBT people. The Church has done such a good job of poisoning the souls of people in regard to homosexuality in particular, that it can stand back and allow us do its dirty work. Although not looking like the most positive step I had taken thus far, my arrival at Dignity was a seismic shift in my path to freedom.

Meanwhile, back in my parish I kept secret my journey downtown Manhattan to the Mass at Dignity. I was popular in the parish of Saint Gabriel's, enjoyed my work there, and so decided to continue my studies beyond my Master's degree. My superiors in Ireland were not at all happy with this decision and ordered me back to our headquarters in Cork city. I refused to go. I could not obey. I was, after all, only at the very beginning of my discovery of who I was and needed desperately the help of my therapist as well as the tentative contacts I had made through Dignity.

When I wrote to my superior and told him that I was only at a 'breakthrough point' of my therapy, he was totally dismissive of my letter. He ordered me home. He said that he had requested a one-way ticket for my journey and that he would see me forthwith for further assignment. I was at my wit's end. What was I going to do now? How was I going to manage my stay, and most importantly how was I going to pay my way for therapy and further studies?

I went to the pastor of the parish and told him my situation. He was empathetic, but deeply opposed to my pursuing doctoral studies in a Protestant seminary. "I don't want any priest in this parish preaching Protestant theology to the people." I had made enquiries and discovered that the New York Theological Seminary on 29th Street and Fifth Avenue offered an interdisciplinary doctorate in ministry, theology, and psychology. This was exactly what I wanted and would satisfy my need for excellence in my academic pursuits, as well as giving me the time and opportunity to work on my emerging gay identity. The seminary while Baptist in origin had an ecumenical faculty.

The journey from self-rejection to self-acceptance is as I have often said a lifetime quest. While I did not confide anything of my inner turmoil to the pastor in charge, I believe he intuited that there was more going on than met the eye. By this time, my pastoral presence in the parish had reached a new high, and I was being sought after for all kinds of talks and lectures in psychology and religion. While I understood the parish priest's desire to rein me in, I could not agree with his sectarianism. I quietly thanked him and started immediately to look for alternative employment. I put the word out that I wished to move from Saint Gabriel's' parish. I placed an advert in the New York Catholic press offering my services.

In the spring of 1978, I was offered and accepted a position as a teacher of religious education at Mount Saint Michael's Academy in the Northeast Bronx. Mount Saint Michael's is a high school for boys, owned and operated by the Marist Brothers of the Schools. At the time of my appointment there was a faculty of thirty-one Religious Brothers and forty lay people. There was an enrolment of 1,300 students. Most of these young men were of Italian and Irish descent with an increasing influx of Latino and African American students.

My contract at the high school was to teach for four days a week as well as making myself available for pastoral work at weekends when necessary. This allowed me one full day every week to be at New York Theological Seminary to pursue my doctoral work. My afternoons, evenings, and some of my weekends I spent on my research. I was delighted with the arrangement and in September 1978, I moved out of rectory living, acquired my own little studio on Broadway and 242nd Street, and began my teaching career at Mount St. Michael's.

This new-found freedom of living on my own was something I had never known before. All my life, I had lived in close quarters with other people and enjoyed very little privacy. Even though my studio was only one room, when I entered it and closed my door it was my palace. I could invite anyone I liked to share my space or be alone whenever I wished. Having been always provided for, both at home and in priesthood, I found cooking, shopping, and laundry a challenge, but it was one I welcomed. Although I was over thirty years of age, I had never signed a cheque. The privilege of the clerical class had emasculated me in more ways than one. I was determined to work for my living and pay my own bills. Until now, utilities like gas, electricity, telephone, and of course food and accommodation had all been provided. I was about to grow up and take care of myself.

Soon after my teaching began at the school, it became obvious to the administration and to me that the pastoral needs on campus were completely overtaking my role as a religious education teacher. The principal asked me if I would be willing to set up a Campus Ministry at the school. To do so he would free me of all teaching assignments. After some thought and discussion with other teachers at the school, I agreed. This new adventure was to become the substance and theoretical basis for my doctoral dissertation later. Having never worked in a high school in New York, this was new territory. I set about building Campus Ministry in the Bronx with that same frame of mind that a priest would have in the 1950s Irish Republic.

The pride and prejudice and the authoritarianism of a full-blooded Irish cleric, were much more mine than I was either conscious of or indeed willing to admit. I was brought up in a home marked by close family ties, a very strict and uncompromising religious ethical atmosphere, and what amounted to a worship of the virtue of hard work All this I took with me when called upon to initiate and facilitate a campus ministry program at a Bronx Catholic high school. The students, as expected, were very different than my own days at secondary school. The first morning I met a group of them, one of them asked, "Father, when did you have sex last?" I was shocked. Thinking on my feet and knowing that this was a litmus test as to 'how cool' I was. I answered, "Do you want me to include last night or not?". . .

I had made it to round two. The word spread and I began to win their trust more and more. I was known affectionately as Padre, and to some of them I would become the only Padre/Father that they would know. I was entrusted with their confidences, joys and pain. To me they brought their problems at home and school – their experimenting with drugs and drink. When they fell in and out of love, I was the first to hear. If one of them got a girl pregnant, they wrongfully presumed I could get them the money for an abortion. When they could not go home, because of family troubles, they would end up on my door step asking to stay the night because, "my father has kicked me out." In many ways I became the 'father' I had always wanted to be and every paternal instinct in me was somewhat satisfied. They became the 'son,' I would never have in real life. I was so happy taking care of them and enjoyed my ministry to them like no other. I never thought it would end.

In time, the Archdiocese of New York recognised my achievement by acknowledging through the publication of their educational offices and their Associate Superintendent of Schools, Father Terry Attridge, that Mount Saint Michael's Academy was the flagship campus ministry programmes in the diocese. The acknowledgement of my work was an accolade I did not expect, but cherished when it arrived. Years later the same archdiocese in a statement from their press officer, Joseph Zwilling, denied that I had ever worked for the diocese.

As I pursued my work at Mount St. Michael's and my doctoral studies, I continued to see my therapist and work at the integration of myself. I was still resisting reality and naively believed that I could marry my Catholic priesthood and my emerging gay sexual identity. I attended Mass regularly at

Dignity and began ever so slowly to identify myself to people I met as well as sharing with them what I did. The ground was taken from under me when one evening I was asked to stand in for a priest who did not turn up to celebrate Mass. I felt under enormous pressure and kept apologising for being so nervous and really having little to say that would be helpful. After all, I was still in the depths of my own self-oppression. I got through it, and people afterwards were overwhelming in their support. Eventually, I agreed to become one of Dignity's regular celebrants.

The board of Dignity/New York used to meet every first Wednesday of the month at the Jesuit residence at West 98th Street and Broadway in Manhattan. This was an apartment block where a Jesuit community from Woodstock – home of the world famous Sixties rock festival - in upstate New York moved when their house in Woodstock closed. The board met to discuss the affairs of the chapter and plan its many pastoral and social activities. Within months of my celebrating Mass for Dignity, I was invited by the board to sit with another priest, Father Bob Carter, SJ, as theological consultant to the board. This marked another step in my coming out process.

I could not accept or understand why my church was so adamant in its opposition to any and all forms of gay liberation. The fact that we had to worship in a non-Catholic Church in a certain sense said it all. Basically, we were not trusted to even congregate together to worship God. God the 'Great Inconvenience' was to change that. We were invited to move our weekly Mass to Saint Francis Xavier Jesuit Church in Greenwich Village. The Village was both the physical - with its many gay bars - and spiritual home to the gay community and was highly appropriate for a pastoral outreach programme to LGBT people. This wonderful baroque church building on West 16th Street near Sixth Avenue became our home for the first and only time in a Catholic church building.

Dan and Dill, two Dignity members, ran a painters and decorators business. They had recently done some work in the Church of Saint Francis for the pastor, Fr. Joe Dirr, SJ. He was so impressed by the work and their integrity as human beings, that when he realised that they were members of Dignity he invited the whole group to come and worship in his Church. The Archdiocese of New York was not happy. In fact, the Chancery Offices at 1011 First Avenue immediately let Father Dirr know that his decision to welcome us was 'a grave mistake'.

These same offices of the New York Archdiocese were once known in New York as 'The Power House.' This was so in the days of Francis Cardinal Spellman and no one ever thought it necessary to change that name. In these same offices of the Archdiocese, all policy for priests and people was decided. The temporal and spiritual power of the Catholic Church in the city of New York was something no one ever questioned. In fact it was common knowledge that the Archdiocese of New York owned more land in the city, than the city itself. On Saint Patrick's Day, every year this great metropolis comes to a stand-still. Catholic school after Catholic school, Catholic colleges and universities, Catholic hospitals - and every department in the city, from the New York Police Department to the New York City Fire Department march past the Cathedral steps as the parade is reviewed by His Eminence the Cardinal. Politicians and Presidential candidates rival one another for prominence in their display of fealty to the Irish Catholic voting public. This great and oldest of New York City parades, is amongst many things a display of Catholic power and triumphalism in the city. No wonder that to this day, the Irish Lesbian Gay organization, are not allowed to march with their co-patriots on this world renowned feast of Irishness. The power of the Church is such that there is still enforced discrimination that the courts or the city seem unwilling to change. One of the few times that I have been physically assaulted, for my human rights work, has been when I choose to march with some protestors against this injustice.

At Saint Francis Xavier's, we as a group of Catholic LGBT people and friends, were home at last. Word spread rapidly, and our numbers increased dramatically. There were on average six hundred people attending our Mass and liturgies every week. This number doubled on feast days like Christmas and Easter and, of course, Gay Pride Day at the end of each June. We became one of the most formidable groups in the city. We had outreach programmes to the homeless, shut-ins, prisoners of Riker's Island, and those who were sick and infirm. After our weekly Mass, we would hold a social hour in the basement of the church where all the various committee's would meet to discuss their services. There was a theatre group, a 'leather and levi' group, and a 'stitch and bitch' group for those interested in crocheting. All tastes were catered for. Many guest speakers of both literary and political renown were invited and accepted to grace our pulpit. I became increasingly more involved with the community and found myself making deep and lasting friendships.

Together with my fellow priests, we formed a support group for one another to enable us to minister to the community. It also gave us a forum to discuss our own struggles in safety and confidentiality. When as priests we decided to lead the Dignity contingent in the gay pride march, we realised we were making a public statement of support for the Catholic LGBT community and their rights. Our passion for justice for our own people was as much motivated by our own inner oppression as it was by our commitment to the Gospel. We made the freedom song of the Reverend Doctor Martin Luther King our own. We sang the Civil Rights anthem 'We Shall Overcome' as we marched up Fifth Avenue, imagining our liberation was only days away. This was the first time I marched as a Catholic priest for human and civil rights for gay people. I would do this for the next thirty years both in New York and London.

When I emerged from the subway at Christopher Street and Sheridan Square in Greenwich Village to join the parade, I could not believe my eyes. There were gay men and lesbians everywhere. There were so many beautiful men, in T-shirts and tank tops, parading with wild abandon and celebration of their identity that I thought I had died and gone to heaven. I wanted everybody in Ireland to be here, especially my family and friends from Ennis. Look, I was saying to myself, I am not the only one. There are thousands of us, lesbian, gay, bisexual and transgendered people. Although I had felt so alone – I was not yet out to my family - on that bright and most memorable day, I was no longer alone. I never would be again.

Journal Entry Number 9

The single most controversial issue for the lesbian/gay community worldwide is same-sex marriage. While our visibility has led to more freedoms being granted to sexual minorities by local and national governments, it has also led to a more raw and virulent opposition. In every country I know violence and physical and verbal against gay people has increased. Nowhere in the West is opposition to LGTB freedom more strongly articulated than in the Catholic Church.

The Church spends millions of Euros in Europe and millions of dollars in the United States to galvanise support for its 'Opposition to Gay Marriage and Civil Partnership'. Is there such an abundance of love in the world that this is necessary? How much more consonant with the Gospel of Jesus Christ were this money to be spent on the 47,000 children who starve to death every day.

Sermon Preached at the Celebratory Mass for Celia Gardiner and Gloria Esperaza Murillo Angel on the Occasion of Their Civil Partnership

'Only through the body does the way, the ascent to the life of blessedness, lie open to us.'

St Bernard of Clairvaux, Sermon on the Song of Songs.

The Song of Songs has long held a privileged place in the mystical theology and monastic tradition of the Church. Commentary on this erotically charged, enigmatic love poetry of the Bible runs like a thread from Origen to St. John of the Cross. It is natural to wonder why the Song of Songs and its erotic imagery informed the spiritual life of so many monastics.

Perhaps no interpretation has exerted a greater influence on Western Christian spirituality than that of St. Bernard of

Clairvaux, whose commentary – 86 sermons composed over a period of 18 years – is rightly revered as a masterpiece of medieval monastic literature. Like many others before and after him, Bernard saw the song as a sublime allegory on the love of God that can be experienced through contemplation. It was the paradigmatic text for monks, because its poetry vividly describes the pursuit that is the basis for the whole programme of monastic life and all life: 'love's union' *with* God, of which the monk may enjoy a sweet foretaste here below.

"Let Him kiss me with kisses of His mouth." Bernard requires no less than seven sermons to expand on this opening verse of the song and to find here an allegory of ascent to the sweetest – indeed, almost sexual – mystical union with Christ the bridegroom, the mediator between the sinner's soul, and the hidden God. Echoing the sensual imagery of the song itself, Bernard provokes the imagination with comparably vivid physical imagery. "How then should you go?" he asks. He invites his hearers to imagine being grasped and bodily lifted out of the mud by the merciful hand of Jesus, and finally drawn to the Lord's mouth, "which is so divinely beautiful, fearing and trembling, not only to gaze on it, but even to kiss it."

The affection Bernard conveys for Jesus here is truly beautiful. "Even the beauty of angels seems tedious to me. For my Jesus outshines them so far in his beauty and loveliness. That is why I ask Him, not any other angel or man, to kiss me with the kiss of His mouth."

'The book of experience', as Bernard called his life, looks different, to say the least for Christians today, especially lesbian, gay, bisexual, and transgendered people. Why must the song, we may well ask, be understood as an allegory of union with God, or in terms that presume a dichotomy between union with God and sexual union with a beloved? Today the more important questions are both theological and psychological: how to plumb the depths of sexuality through the eyes of God, the divine artist who fashioned it, and where possible to let the mystery be deepened through meditation on scripture itself.

Without diminishing the riches that have been gathered from allegorical readings of the Song of Songs, one may still insist on the value of a more literal reading for us. The Catholic Christian has less to fear and much more to celebrate in the God-given mystery of human sex, rightly and reverently embraced. Surely same-gender sexual relationships may be one of the best-kept secrets in the sacramental life of the Church, to be ranked among the Church's most sacred objects. Before recoiling from this perhaps surprising statement and draining its force with a thousand qualifications, we ought to think about the thousands of millions of hidden saints who like Celia and Gloria here today discover some part of their own stumbling sanctity in lover relationships.

The following is a section of a twelfth-century love poem, of which there are many, by two German nuns from a convent in the Rhineland, Southern Germany:

"To G. her unique rose
A. sends the bond of precious love."

"Much strength have I that I may bear your absence. Is my strength the strength of stones that I can wait for your return? I never cease from aching night and day, like someone missing a hand or foot. Without you anything happy and delightful seems like mud trod underfoot. Instead of rejoicing I weep. My spirit never seems joyful. When I remember the kisses you gave me. The way you refreshed my little breasts with sweet words, I would like to die since I can no longer see you. If my body had been committed to earth until you're longed for return, or if I could go on a journey like Habbakuk, so that just once I saw the face of my lover, then I would not care if I died that very hour. There is no one born into this world as lovable and dear as you.

No one who loves me with so deep a love. I ache without end until I am allowed to see you." (See *Christian, Social Tolerance and Homosexuality* by John Boswell, University of Chicago Press, 1980. Also, *Same Sex Unions* by John Boswell. New York, Villard Books, 1994.)

In lover relationships like this, many pilgrims meet beauty: the luminous landscape of the lover's body, the rise of the shoulder blade, the bowl of the navel, the curve of the lips, and myriad other primordial shapes pressing and receiving like the roll and tumble of fecund nature. By sharing with each other this dance of play and joy and gratitude, lovers give glory to God by being in that moment precisely whom God wants them to be. Here, as Merton might say, 'their inscape is their sanctity'.

It is in loving relationships like the one we celebrate today that many pilgrims meet knowledge, the grace of coming to know another deeply, and being known, not through heroic effort and applied technique, but through slow-paced trust, honesty, friendship, and grace.

In Christian terms, sexual love is a manifestation of the Incarnation – its goodness revealed not just in spite of our sinfulness, but because of it. To say it more personally: it is the lover's acceptance, affection, and sheer delight in the beloved that—perhaps more than any force—sets one free from failings and teaches one the gratuitous nature of divine love.

Yet experience has taught Catholics to be wary of their own myths. Highly idealized notions of 'Christian marriage' can be just as illusory and damaging to people today as idealized perceptions of the celibate life have been in the past. Should we not be able to celebrate the God-given goodness of sex and sexuality – and the vocation to celibacy or the single life – without staking out a dangerous caste system? The seriousness of these difficulties, made worse by the cultural wars of our own time here in the United Kingdom, threatens to cloud the waters around sexuality so badly that we lose all confidence in the credibility of the tradition. Above all, it must not be forgotten that the Catholic view of sex rests in the biblical vision of creation itself: 'It is very good.' The Song of Songs can help us to inform ourselves and our lesbian, gay, bisexual and transgendered children in that tradition.

If St. Bernard's account of the spiritual life is anything, it is holistic: "Only through the body does the way, the ascent to the life of blessedness, lie open to us." This profound intuition—the fruit of an incarnational faith—permits us to welcome in the mystery of sex more than an echo of the final joy of heaven. Especially for those in relationship or desirous of relationship, meditation on the Song of Songs can nurture both gratitude for the gift of love's union now and a shimmering hope for the reign of God yet to come.

Let us not overlook the prophetic and sign-bearing power of sexual love right now, on this side of history. The woman and woman, man and man, or woman and man who delight in each other, though fragile and hidden in the general cosmic dance, lie together in the margins and shine like a silver moon in a dark night sky. Their whole being echoes the sublime refrain of the Song of Songs: "Deep waters cannot quench love, nor floods sweep it away."

We celebrate with joy and gratitude that perennial truth of Celia and Gloria today.

We wish you joy in that which of its nature is joyful. And a profound sorrow in that which of its nature is sorrowful.

For both are beautiful. Beautiful are your hearts, for having found God in both.

Feast of Our Lady of Lourdes 2006

Autumn

Then the unimaginable and inconceivable happened! AIDS struck like a plague from hell. The party was over. At first, there was total denial that anything serious was happening. After all, to think that sex could kill was beyond the mind and imagination of most twentieth-century people. Venereal disease was always a possibility and no one seriously thought of themselves invulnerable to disease. Yet to be struck down by a life-threatening illness at a time of our adolescence as a gay community was completely off the radar. It seemed like the revenge of the God of fire and brimstone preached to us by the Redemptorists (a Catholic religious order renowned throughout Ireland in the 1950s and 1960s for their hell-fire sermons, especially against sins of the flesh). Not surprisingly, the first statement from the Vatican on AIDS—by Monsignor (now Archbishop) John Patrick Foley—was that we brought this disease on ourselves.

At first no one knew how the disease was spread. Everyone who was gay considered themselves as a possible target. More and more people were falling sick from unknown or very rare forms of diseases. The first name given the disease was GRID (Gay Related Immune Deficient Syndrome). As close friends began to get very ill and die of the most horrible opportunistic infections, everyone in the community became paranoid. Who is next? Will it be me? There were all kinds of rumours going around as to whom the angel of death would strike next and how the disease was contacted. People's lives ran wild with fear and paranoia. "Can I catch it from a toilet seat, or touching someone, or drinking from the same chalice for Communion at Mass?" people asked.

At a Dignity Mass in the fall of 1982, in fear and desperation, I called a meeting to rally the community to help in caring for the most ill and dying. Many gay people left the city returning to their home of origin thinking that they were going to die there.

Professional people, like some doctors, nurses, and hospital orderlies, were afraid to touch the sick in case they became contaminated with the disease. Often, on visiting friends and people in need at different hospitals, we found patients' food was found left outside the doors of their wards, as the orderlies feared to enter the room in case they too caught whatever was causing this scourge. Many people were left alone to die. I was shocked, horrified, and angry beyond words.

Dignity AIDS ministry attracted increasingly more people, some now ill with the virus, and others wanting to help in whatever way they could. The city mayor, Edward Koch, formed a Task Force on AIDS. I was drafted onto this group as a representative of the Catholic gay community and Dignity AIDS Ministry. Gradually, more of my time was being spent in caring for the sick, assisting the dying, and burying the dead. Churches closed their doors to receiving the remains of the deceased before burial for funeral Mass or Requiem. They too feared contamination and, of course, because HIV/AIDS was first named as the 'gay plague' there was little sympathy. Many clerics did not hide their belief that we 'queers' were getting what we deserved. Reddens Funeral Home at 14th Street in Greenwich Village was the first place to show a welcome for the remains of those who died. It became both chapel and funeral parlour for the dead and bereaved.

There was much confusion, great ignorance, and horrendous prejudice in certain powerful quarters. The White House, where the very conservative and anti-gay Ronald Reagan Administration was in power, simply ignored the growing epidemic. Reagan himself did not speak publicly about AIDS until seven years into the epidemic by which time it was out of control and spreading worldwide.

The *New York Times*, the paper of record, failed completely to report what was going on. After a hugely successful fundraiser for people sick and dying of the disease at Barnum and Baileys

Circus in Madison Square Garden, the *New York Times* gave what was happening in our community front-page headlines. This was subsequent to a 'Paper Burning' initiative taken by the gay community as a form of protest against the *Times'* lack of coverage of the epidemic.

Larry Kramer, one of our most strident and formidable leaders, and his friends started a grass-roots organisation in 1981 called Gay Men's Health Crisis (GMHC) to provide advocacy and care, which is in existence to this very day. The Archdiocese of New York simply buried its head in the sand. Slowly through the public protest of groups such as the radical Act Up, also founded by Kramer in 1987, things improved, services became more accessible, and promising treatments were fast-tracked by the Food and Drug Administration. This, of course, was greatly helped by the medical discovery that HIV, the virus discovered as the cause of AIDS in 1984, was transmitted through blood, semen and vaginal fluids.

While services improved at a city level, the sheer bigotry felt by people with the virus did not let up. In fact, as the disease became more widely known and publicised, prejudice increased. This was sadly most often the case for those unfortunate fellow-Catholics who were ill. Fellow-priests of mine – with the virus – were often shunned by their diocese and religious communities. Parents and families took their lead from the scandalous example their Church gave them. Parents all too frequently were full of shame and pain as they discovered for the first time that their son was not only gay but also dying from the gay plague.

Eventually, the Church too did respond to the crisis. New York's John Cardinal O'Connor with Mother Teresa opened a hospice for the sick and dying. This was called, Gift of Love, and run by the Missionary Sisters of the Poor. This is Mother Teresa's own Religious Order. We were delighted by this turn of events, although not for long. Our friends who were inmates were forbidden to have their lovers, friends, or life partner's visit. The sick and dying were often forced to confess their sinful lifestyle and renounce the very love that was central to their existence. I was outraged.

This kind of shocking injustice was not only true in New York, but in different and diverse ways in so many towns and cities the world over. In Ennis, the town of my birth, no one has 'officially' died of HIV/AIDS. I personally know of three people who in fact have succumbed to the disease in the town. Cancer or some other 'acceptable' disease was and is always used as a cover in such cases. Young men denied not only the reality of their lives but also their deaths. There are exceptions to this, but they remain exceptions. When contacted by our AIDS ministry team regarding their critically ill son, a typical response from many parents was, 'You take care of him. We don't want to know.' Or worse still, 'Find a grave and bury him.' More ashes of 'unknown soldiers' went into the Hudson River at the bottom of Christopher Street in Greenwich Village New York than I care to remember. Camus's Plague was reality.

Unrepeatable as my first Gay Pride march was, it is not my most unforgettable. That was to come years later. During the late spring 1984, at the height of the HIV/AIDS pandemic, the media was saturated with news of Mayor Koch's new Executive Order 50. This initiative was introduced by the Mayor to stop discrimination against lesbian and gay people by employers who received city funding. In other words, the gay community's taxes were not to be used to discriminate against us in employment.

The Catholic Archdiocese of New York, under the new leadership of Archbishop John O'Connor, was vehemently opposed to the legislation. At that time the Archdiocese, as stated elsewhere, held more property in its possession in New York than the city itself. It was powerfully wealthy. Its arms stretched everywhere with churches, schools, hospitals orphanages, and tracts of the most valuable land right across the city boundaries. The Archdiocese did receive millions of dollars of city money to help finance its many and varied social programmes in the city. Given the track record of the Catholic Church in relationship to gay people, it came as no great surprise that it opposed the most basic of human rights in our regard.

At the Gay Pride Parade in1984, Dignity New York as usual marched with thousands of others on the last Sunday in June to commemorate Stonewall and celebrate our freedom and thirst for justice as lesbian, gay, and transgendered people. The name Stonewall is the name of the gay bar in Greenwich Village that was routinely closed down by the New York Police Department. Its patrons were always hassled, beaten, treated like dirt, and eventually carted off in police vans for simply gathering together in the same place. In 1969, the patrons decided they had enough dehumanising treatment by the police and fought back in three nights of riots and rebellion. By doing so, they gave birth to the modern gay liberation movement.

The board of directors of Dignity New York elected me in 1984 to lead our group of LGBT Catholics in the Gay Parade in prayer. This was to be done on the steps of St Patrick's Cathedral as the parade passed us by. The Dignity contingent would leave the parade on approaching Saint Patrick's Cathedral on 52nd Street and prayerfully gather for a few moments of silence. I was instructed to lead the recitation of the Our Father or Lord's Prayer as a statement of our common faith and commitment to justice and co-equality for all people.

As expected, I was dressed in my Roman collar for the occasion. Having completed my task, I descended the steps of the Cathedral and found myself suddenly surrounded by press reporters and television cameras. Microphones were shoved in my face as I was asked, "Father, what is your response to Mayor Koch's Executive Order 50 forbidding discrimination against lesbian-gay people in matters of employment?" I answered simply, "Employment is a basic human right for all people; women, men, black, white, gay and heterosexual." On being asked further whether this would in any way contravene Catholic Church teaching, I answered that "justice for all is at the very heart of the Gospel message."

Without my realizing it, this was to be my baptism by fire. The lead story on that evening's news on all the major stations was in one way or another, "Catholic Priest Opposes Archbishop." AIDS deaths in our community had reached epidemic proportions, and I was already feeling burnout, even though it would be 'a long day's journey into night' before there would be any respite. Time does not change events, but it can with the objectivity of distance change how we understand them. This 'coming out' in the New York media for the equality of my own people was a must for me.

In light of the most ignominious suffering I was witnessing first hand as I saw brother after brother die of AIDS, I was learning more about God, sex, power, and death than I ever wanted to know. Yes, way back as a little boy in Ennis, I too had heard the sound of another drummer. In different and diverse ways, I had either ignored or muted that voice within me, hiding behind my Roman collar, family, fear, and so on. This was to be no more. Eventually the word *courage* lost meaning, as so much was taken away. I can only say I am grateful, most of all to those who taught me so much as they made their last journey through death to what I hope is new life. They are the ones who spared no price and counted no cost and their names are legion.

Journal Entry Number 10

Antonio

I remember a Friday, my 'usual' night with Antonio.

"Antonio, I do so much enjoy our Friday evenings together," I said. "Well I hope you can forgive me if some Friday I am not there." And then he laughed that loud, full laugh of his. It was emphatic and sincere with a touch of cynicism. He laughed at the foibles of the world – and at his own. He could forgive the world, but he rarely could forgive himself. He was an optimistic man - well at least a hopeful one. If he had lost hope in himself, he recognized it in others and respected it. He respected me.

I watched Antonio die. I watched out for him during his final stay in hospital. I fought with the nurses; I fought with the doctors. They wouldn't listen to him. They'd dismissed him as incompetent and saw him as a 'difficult' patient. He was.

Antonio melted away while his brilliant, pithy, creative mind crumbled and decomposed. On the glaze of his eyes, a nightmare danced. His voice was a rumble, a needle on a scratchy record. His words painted horror. From such fragments he had to make his way when the sky was so very dark.

I was able to understand him, when the doctors could not. I could understand him when he asked for water, when he needed help to urinate, and when he wanted salve for his Kaposi. When he shit himself, I tried to be light hearted and say with grave irreverence, that being Catholic had taught me how to deal with a lot of shit! He tried to laugh.

It took Antonio a long time to convey a complete thought or a complete message. Doctors can only understand complete sentences. Antonio no longer spoke in complete sentences.

He told me he wanted to die. There were no 'good' moments anymore, he said. "Life was only one big pain in the ass; not the kind I enjoy." He pressed me to help him kill himself. I can still see the intensity in his eyes through the penetrating gaze of his skull. It looked like a death camp caricature of a face. "Please, help me please."

This was August 1986, before AZT, before anything. There was not even the shred of hope. There was nowhere to hide. Death stared us in the face. Late that August I left the city to take the final week of a planned three-week vacation. With a friend, I had rented a cottage by the sea, in the middle of nowhere, somewhere on the coast of Maine, not far from Provincetown.

I wrote to the Hemlock Society for information. The plan was that, when I returned, Antonio would sign himself out of the hospital, and I would help him die at home. Somehow I knew that there was no way that he was going to walk out of that hospital. On the Sunday of that weekend I was entertaining friends, and at 3.00 p.m., we were talking about Antonio. On Monday morning I made my daily call to the hospital to discover that Antonio had died on Sunday afternoon.

Antonio gave me two suit jackets, a dark blue one and a grey one. We were the same size, although Antonio was taller. I liked wearing Antonio's clothes. When I used to do HIV/AIDS funerals, I would wear one of Antonio's jackets. Wearing his jacket gave me strength to carry on.

He was a unique man, full of colour, and we often disagreed. We sometimes did not speak to each other for days. He was an iconoclast. I often thought that he was mad. He returned the compliment. He could make me laugh and send me up when my seriousness about the Church got too much.

He was a role model for young gays. They gave him their toughness, their naivety, and their frailty. They came from the American heartland, seeking freedom in New York City. They were runaways, throwaways, castaways of America's Christian parents. Antonio could not heal their pain, but he often gave them the strength to be able to live with it. He gave them a belief in their own unique goodness. More importantly, Antonio gave them practical street smarts. He wasn't a Lower East Side Italian New Yorker for nothing.

Antonio had a fantasy. He wanted to open a residence for homeless gay youths—a place of refuge for betrayed children. Antonio was self-sufficient and fiercely independent. He had an artist's sense of the world with an ability to negotiate in order to pay the rent. He saw himself as a failed artist. He never forgave himself for not achieving his dream. He felt that the promise of his youth was unfulfilled.

He was only thirty-two years of age when he passed away. His spirit was never broken. His spirit was subversive and mischievous. It taunted a disease that eventually killed him. Yet he himself endured. He was himself to the end. He was alive when he died. How much better than to be dead and survive.

Once during those final weeks of his illness, he picked up his dick between his two fingers and shook it at me, "Worthless!" For Antonio being gay was many things – politics, brotherhood, community, survival, culture, life, creativity, spirituality and sex. He was angry that AIDS stole all of this. He has gone from erection to Resurrection. Rest well my friend.

Autumn Continues

By May 1980, I had completed my doctoral degree and, after a three-month sabbatical, returned to my campus ministry work. I spent most of the three months with my friend Jeremy in London. He was in the process of leaving the ordained ministry to try as he said, "to put my life together."

On a visit to New York in summer 1978, he had confided in me that he too had been 'struggling with his homosexuality all of his priestly life.' It was this, as much as his genuine compassion that had enabled him to empathise with Jay and me in seminary and consequently not follow 'the party line'. Of course, I also discovered much later that he was deeply in love with me as his student and that his question, 'Have you ever entered each other from behind?' was as he put it in a letter I still have in my possession 'a way of holding onto me'. I was shocked when he told me these things as I never suspected for one moment that the greatest hero of my seminary training could 'fall in love' with me.

Eventually, in the fall of 1980, Jeremy decided to move to New York. I was able to secure him a position in the counselling department of the academy, and with the help of some friends furnished my studio apartment for him in the Northwest Bronx. I moved to a one bedroom a little distance away.

I very much enjoyed my work at the school, and having my dearest friend, Jeremy, there was an added bonus. As I became increasingly more involved in AIDS ministry my work at the school not only paid my bills but also gave me a welcome respite from the sick and dying. Jeremy did not take part in the ministry, but was greatly supportive of my work. He too became a weekly participant at our Mass for LGBT people at St Francis Xavier, and through it he made some good friendships of love and support. I was very happy for him. I loved him dearly, but we were never lovers.

With all the coming and going I failed to notice Jeremy's

declining health until he brought it to my attention. Jeremy was not happy at Mount St Michael's Academy. His academic career had been in third level education. Although grateful to the Marist Brothers for employing him, working as a counsellor to freshmen in a Catholic high school was a step down professionally for this highly educated, intelligent, and gifted man. Until his Green Card came through, however, nothing else was on offer.

Like so many, Jeremy saw New York differently from the way he had imagined it from Dublin and London. The truth was that being away from Ireland was a bitter pill for him to swallow. He found the challenge of daily life and work in the city quite daunting. I was used to listening to him air his difficulties as we travelled back and forth to school together every day. By this time, I was settled and had fallen deeply in love with New York. I had acquired my own automobile, which was necessary for my work. In a sense, there may have been some sibling rivalry between us. Jeremy always had been my mentor and my senior. Out of my love and respect for him I always deferred to him and had in fact dedicated my doctoral thesis to him. Now the relationship was somewhat reversed.

I tried as best I could to honour his needs, but I could not replace the power and priesthood from which he had chosen to leave. For Jeremy there could be no reconciliation between his gayness and his priesthood. To him they were totally incompatible. As he became more and more aware of his sexual orientation he wanted to apply for laicization. Both our Provincial superior at the time and I agreed that this was not the way forward. Jeremy, although alienated like so many of his gay confreres from the institutional Church, was not alienated from his faith in God or Christ. He attended daily Mass in the student chapel. I used to celebrate Mass for the faculty and student body in both Lent and Advent. He loved to discuss theology, and during such discourse, he would once again become the professor of great insight and deepest humility to whom I remain indebted.

Although we were closer than close, I never questioned him about his sexual life. I knew he had one, and we occasionally skimmed around it. When initially he said he was not feeling well and not sleeping because of night sweats, I did not think for one moment that it might have anything to do with AIDS. As his health declined, and he looked truly awful with little energy, I accepted his story that 'the doctor thought he might have lymphoma'.

In spring 1982, my parents came to visit me in New York for the first time. Not since Cleopatra went up the Nile to meet Mark Anthony had there been such excitement. My mother was on such a high that I thought she had dropped a tab of ecstasy. Everyone in both my school and former parish wanted to meet Mom and Dad, entertain them, and show them the sights of New York. I was delighted for them.

Jeremy also took part in the round of celebrations and hospitality. He knew them well as he had often stayed with them during his visits to Ennis. Although he was 'not himself' as my mother observed he was still as gracious and kind as ever. We were on Easter vacation during most of their trip. Having taken them to visit relatives in Florida, I had to return to New York for work before them. Jeremy volunteered to look after my parents on their return as I had a scheduled retreat in upstate New York with a junior class at Mount St Michael's.

On my return from the retreat they praised Jeremy for his wonderful cooking skills and boasted about the great time he gave them during my absence. They returned to Ireland a week later. That was the last time they and Jeremy would see each other. My mother passed away suddenly the following September. During that most painful episode, my friend was most truly my friend.

Journal Entry Number 11

The loss of my mother created in me an absence that has never been filled. She was so tied in with my faith and priesthood that it is difficult for me to separate the two. I have no doubt in saying that, in a certain sense, I did have 'my mother's vocation'. I also have, of course, my own. I do not know where I would be in my vocation if she were alive. I do know that her absence was and is conduit to the 'road less travelled' that I have taken.

In Memory of My Mother, 1 September 1982

My mother is dead. This event cannot claim uniqueness. It is among the most common of human experiences. Few sons and daughters have not experienced or will not experience the death of their mother, suddenly or slowly, far away or close by. Yet, it is in the usual, normal, and ordinary events that we touch the mystery of human life. What is most universal is also most personal. In life, she belonged to a few. In death she belongs to all.

As I flew from New York Kennedy to Shannon airport, a journey I had made so many times before, I realised that I was going to say farewell to my mother. As often as I had taken this trip, this time it seemed unreal. Already I felt my perceptions changing as my immediate surroundings seemed to fade away. Above the cold North Atlantic I felt alone: not lonely, not depressed, not anxious, not afraid, but alone in a new way. My mother was dead. She would not be waiting for me at home in Ennis, to welcome me with the warm and sensuous kiss that I had come to know and love.

Her eyes, in which love and sadness were never completely separate, taught me from the beginning that there is no living in love without pain. From her, I had come to feel an unqualified acceptance that had little to do with my being good or bad, successful or unsuccessful, close by or far away. In her I had begun to sense a love that was free from demands and manipulations, a love that gave me a sense of belonging that could be found nowhere else. She represented a reality of goodness and safety that was much larger than her. She knew me, accepted me, and wished only for my happiness.

She gave me the basic sense of the goodness of life that allowed me to move freely and fearlessly to many places, to live with many different people and in many different circumstances, and to feel free far from home. The bond between us, which she had created, had grown stronger and deeper over the years. Our relationship now had moved into the realm of memory.

The saddest moment was my arrival at our home in 3, Saint Michael's Villas. I did not dare look at my father. We both understood that she would not be present. She would not open the door and embrace me. She would not invite us to table and pour tea. It was an empty house, not home for me anymore. Everything that for years had spoken of her presence now reminded me of her absence. Everything that had always told me she was at home now told me I would never hear her warm voice again. She who had written to me weekly since I had left home, as a teenager, would never write again.

I celebrated Holy Mass for her, my mother, who had evoked in me the desire to become a priest.

Late Autumn

In the academic year of 1982/3, Jeremy's general health and psychological well-being continued to deteriorate. By this time he had found an excellent Jesuit psychotherapist. I continued to assume that his physiological deterioration was due to the lymphoma for which he told me he was being treated. He informed me that he was seriously considering returning to the Society of African Missions. He had been invited to teach in their seminary in Dedham, near Boston. Knowing how unhappy he was as a counsellor at Mount Saint Michael's Academy I encouraged him to do so.

He cleared out his studio giving most of his furnishings to two young gay lovers he had met in Dignity. His brother Bruce would later try to sue them for 'illegal possession' of his brother's gift. Jeremy would for now do supply work in a local parish until the seminary year began in September. Meanwhile I decided to return to Ireland for my usual summer vacation. The long vacations were one of the great bonus points of teaching, and I took full advantage to get out of my adopted city's sweltering humidity. Jeremy wrote to me in Ireland from his parish. I still possess the letter in which he stated, "I would rather have AIDS of the body than the AIDS of the mind some of these priests have that I am living with. They are totally fucked up."

On my return to New York after my summer vacation in Europe, Jeremy came to stay with me. I shall never forget seeing him approach me along the gangway at La Guardia airport. He looked like a walking skeleton, a living coat hanger, or an escapee from one of the concentration camps one sees so often in movies about the holocaust. Jeremy said nothing to enlighten me other than he 'was getting better'.

Later on in the week I took Jeremy to Rye Beach, New York. While I swam he sat in sombre silence under an umbrella out of the sun's glare. When I came out of the water I asked him, if he were worried about his health and he said that he was, but confident that he would be fine... He then went on to raise our favourite topic, theology. On this occasion, he seemed to be most concerned about the theology of resurrection and afterlife. He did not present, as was his style, any absolute arguments. The only absolute for Jeremy, as he taught me as a young student, was love. He argued cogently that life beyond death was the bedrock of faith in Jesus Christ. Using the Apostle John's first epistle, he said, in most typical Jeremy fashion, that "we know we shall pass from death to life, because we love."

It was only after he had passed on that the force of those words hit me like a thunderbolt from on high. After his stay in New York, Jeremy returned to the African Missions House in Dedham, Massachusetts. He was not long there before he was admitted to Boston General Hospital. I returned to my work at the school and continued to minister to those sick and dying of AIDS.

I was in a total state of denial about Jeremy's condition. I can now see with the benefit of hindsight, that I did not wish to know that my mentor and dearest friend was dying: a man and priest I deeply and dearly loved and admired; someone who I knew was barely out of the closet and had to my knowledge very little sexual experience. Jeremy just could not have AIDS, I told myself. It was impossible! 'There are none as blind as those who do not wish to see'.

I stayed in regular contact with him by phone. Every weekend I took the airline shuttle from New York La Guardia to Boston Logan airport to visit him at Boston General. He seemed to be stabilising, and on my visits we both put on a good face. During that fall of 1983, my Aunt Ethna visited from Ireland. She has always been my favourite aunt. She had met Jeremy on many occasions during his visits to Ennis. She wanted to see him, and so we both went to Boston to visit. Afterwards she lovingly impressed on me that 'it would take a miracle' to get Jeremy back on his feet.

Nearing Christmas, when I saw Jeremy in Boston General, he said that his brother Bruce, a priest in Florida, had invited him for the Christmas vacation and that he intended to go. I was surprised, given the present state of his health and the real reservations Jeremy had as to whether Bruce would accept him as a gay man, but Jeremy was determined. He said the break would do him good and might help him to get better. His doctor said he believed Jeremy would be able to travel. I told him that seeing he was not going to be on the east coast, I would go and spend Christmas with my sister Mary and her husband Richard in Dublin.

On my return from Ireland after the holidays I immediately rang his brother in Florida. I was most anxious to find out how Jeremy was doing. His brother's secretary told me that Jeremy was in hospital and that I should call back later. I went to school very troubled about the state of Jeremy's health. I telephoned again from my office to determine whether I should fly to Florida. Again, Bruce was not available, but if I called at lunchtime then I would certainly catch him in. I called at lunch time!

Nothing in heaven or earth prepared me for the tirade of venom and abuse that Father Bruce poured out over the phone. He told me that Jeremy was very ill and unable to speak to anyone. He ranted and raved about 'the lifestyle' we led, and how he knew 'everything' about me and the priests from Dignity. He warned me not to come near the hospital or he would have the police evict me.

I was shaking when I came off the phone and did not know what to do. At first I went into denial, explanation, and justification for what had transpired on the phone. I told myself that Bruce was in shock and overwrought by the experience of his brother's deteriorating health. I contacted our provincial superior in Cork, Ireland, and filled him in on the situation. I prayed as I have never prayed before for that miracle my Aunt Ethna had talked about on her visit to Jeremy in Boston.

On the evening of 17 January 1984 I had a telephone call from one of Jeremy's sister's in London to tell me that my dearest friend had died. I was so numbed by the news that I continued to work. I had scheduled to see some private patients for psychotherapy and did so as if nothing had happened.

Jeremy's body was to be returned to New York and flown back to Ireland where he would be buried in the family cemetery, in County Sligo. This was in direct contradiction to his explicit wish to be buried with his confreres in the African Missions cemetery, in Wilton, Cork. I was told by my provincial that it was in my best interests not to attend funeral or burial.

Eventually, when the awful truth of what had happened began to sink in, I did not know what to do with my ineffable pain and sadness. I telephoned my father in Ireland. He knew Jeremy very well, and I had kept him and my family up to date about Jeremy's deteriorating health. He said that he and my brothers Sean and Patrick would go to the funeral. My sister Mary and her husband would go to Dublin airport to meet 'the remains', and both my father and sister would be in touch. I did what I always do under great stress; I went for a long run.

After the funeral, I telephoned my father, to hear about Jeremy's final farewell. He told me, with deep emotion that is unusual for him to express, that it had "indeed been a very sad occasion;" but "saddest of all," Jeremy's brother Father Bruce berated the Society of African Missions during the Requiem Mass 'for not taking better care of his brother'. The Society, to my knowledge, had in fact done all that they could and more to care for Jeremy. Our superiors had in their dealings with Jeremy and me shown great patience and compassionate concern during the time of his deteriorating health. I still did not understand what was bothering Father Bruce.

Meanwhile, I tried to get on with my life as best I could. My daily work at Mount Saint Michael's, together with my growing pastoral ministry to people living and dying with HIV and AIDS kept me busy. I was distracted from what was my overwhelming grief. I was distraught at not having been able to see Jeremy before he died. Having been 'forced' to stay away from his funeral only compounded my pain and sense of total alienation. I still believed that Jeremy had died of cancer of the lymph nodes. Some teachers in the school started a rumour that Jeremy must have died of AIDS. I was shocked and posted a public notice up denying this.

One week later, I was called to the American headquarters of the Society of African Missions in Tenafly, New Jersey. For the first time I learnt of the true cause of Jeremy's passing. Father Ulick, my SMA confrere, informed me that Jeremy had indeed died of AIDS. His brother's unmitigated anger toward me and the Society was because, in Bruce's mind, we were to blame for Jeremy's infection with the AIDS virus. Everything began to fall into place. Later my colleague Brother Tom Long, the head of the counselling department for which Jeremy had worked at Mount Saint Michael's Academy, confirmed that Jeremy had confided in him that he had AIDS. Brother Tom had been requested by Jeremy not to share the information with me and had in fact been sworn to secrecy. Jeremy, it seems, did not want me to know, as he believed I too might have the HIV virus. Thankfully, he was wrong. I was now more upset than ever. But there was worse to come.

Journal Entry Number 12

The Millport Experience

In the late 1980s, Steve Retson had written to me in New York, inviting me to come and share my experience of working with HIV and AIDS with the Scottish AIDS Monitor (SAM). I had never been to Scotland, and consequently it was with a sense of both adventure and apprehension that I arrived in Glasgow in October 1991. My nervousness on arrival was very soon allayed. I was greeted at Glasgow Central Station by Ken Cowan, John McClelland, Jamie McTaggart, and Edith Cambell. The warmth of their welcome was enough to put any born again New Yorker totally at ease.

After my experiences of HIV/AIDS in New York, I was being invited to lead what was called 'The Millport/Cumbrae Experience'. Over the next ten years, every four months or so, a group of us ranging in numbers from sixteen to thirty-two people would leave Glasgow on a Friday afternoon for the Isle of Cumbrae, returning on the following Sunday. Those participating in the group experience ranged in age from nineteen years to mid-seventies. They were of all sexual and religious persuasions, including those who did not identify with any religion or sexual grouping. We had one thing in common. We were to a person either HIV positive or deeply affected by the disease. The workshops aimed to provide a safe space where people either infected or affected could deal with the reality of their situation without judgement or fear.

In New York in the early 1980s, when GRID (Gay Related Immune Deficient Syndrome, as it was known then) hit us with the force of an atomic blast, we had no way of articulating the incomprehensible and unimaginable devastation and loss it brought in its wake. Consequently, we devised a form of mime, called para-theatrics, that enabled and empowered us to act out what it is was we were feeling inside at the sudden and awful realisation of our own mortality. At Millport, the meaninglessness of such young and horrifically painful death in our midst, reminded us that all the efforts mainstream society uses to prop itself up with matters of consequence and to pretend its values and aims are so important, are nonsense. Such proximity to death brought us face to face with one fact: all the striving for riches and fame, stability and security that obsess most of us most of the time are ultimately doomed. Through our honest and open sharing, we came to realise that all that remained was this: here we are, each of us, pent into peculiar difficulties, with which we must struggle.

Some moments teach us the price of the human connection. Millport was such a moment. We learnt anew that the difference of social position, intellect, culture, or religion that different people exhibit and on which they so fantastically pin their pride are so small as practically to vanish. We became more lovingly aware than ever before of the depths of worth that lay hidden in each person's life.

Confidentiality was imperative for the process to work. We tried to deal with whatever came up for us personally and collectively. When we surfaced from our shared pain, the joy, freedom, and love experienced were transparently credible and enriching. No one will ever forget the Saturday night parties. The extraordinary display of talent left Broadway and the West End in the shade. The journey back to Laargs and then Glasgow on the Sunday afternoon was a genuine high of true human celebration and freedom.

The backdrop of spirituality and sexuality as a dialectic for the weekend was to my mind what made the time there so passionate, compassionate, painful, and joyful. We all I believe grew up in a world where with Simon and Garfunkel we intuited, 'God had His hand on us all' and 'our backs were to the wall'. We swallowed whole the belief that if we were ever to have a true spirituality, then our sexuality had to be oppressed, repressed, and suppressed at any and every cost.

In Cumbrae, we discovered that our spirituality and sexuality were already one. Their separateness is an illusion encouraged and endorsed primarily by organised religion. This recognition of our slavery and oppression was the first step to freedom.

As the bird breaks its shell from the inside, so we too must grow from within. A person becomes what she or he is open to. To be open to love in such pain as HIV/AIDS we had to be ready to go to the desert where the dark reveals life as mystery, as nothingness, and as emptiness. 'The desert' we found on Cumbrae was the place of encounter with death, freedom, and love incomprehensible. As all structures fell apart, we uncovered and discovered often for the first time that we had 'nothing to fear but fear itself.'

The true self is like a shy wild animal. It only comes out in the stillness when we have given up all pretences of being in control. Our truest self is love eternal; our true selves are God.

Throughout our weekends we came into our spiritualities/ sexualities still in pain and still struggling into the light. The touchstone of who we are is an absolute point of nothingness. This is the point without illusion. The place of poverty and exile became the pure glory of God in us. Those who were in exile often came home to themselves. They discovered that they belonged to the universe. Sexuality and spirituality became one. Free of fear, we became one with the river. As thirty-two-year-old Michael said on his last Cumbrae experience a few weeks before he died, "Acceptance, I have discovered is all. Acceptance is everything."

In our darkest winters at Millport we found an invincible springtime. For what could we hope? Our honour, our experience, our intelligence told us that freedom, not happiness, is the precious stone. One cannot cling to happiness. Happiness submits to no clinging. In Millport over the years and the many workshops we shared, we learnt that ultimately life is gift. Everything is gift. There is nothing to be achieved by clinging. Freedom, not happiness, is the pearl of great price. The freedom to be grateful for what life delivers. The greatest freedom is the freedom to let go, and let life be.

Deep Winter

For a very long time, I had wanted to write about what happened inside of me since the Trial and all that went before. For reasons that I hope shall become more obvious, I could not. While I am aware that much has been written by the media and me (*A Priest On Trial*, Bloomsbury Publishing, 1994) about 'the event', it has taken all this time for me to even begin to look on the inside and share what I see. In this process it is painfully obvious that the history, which produces us, cannot be given away. Yet there are some moments in life, and they needn't be many, or at the time seem that important, that can make up for so much in that life, can redeem, justify the injustice, the bewilderment with which we all live, investing us with the courage not only to endure, but to profit from it. I believe that this is such a moment.

When I arrived in London in the early spring of 1992 there wasn't a bone in the soul of my body that had been left unbroken. In the preceding ten years I had lost friends, lovers, and mentors to the AIDS virus. I had endured the most ignominious witch-hunt culminating in a very public trial, forcing a self-imposed exile from the city that I loved. In fact, during one of my many public lectures at that time, I described my soul as looking like a bombed out castle amongst whose ruins I now live, in a makeshift tent at the mercy of the elements.

While my head understood what was happening, my heart collapsed into total despair and absolute fear of everyone and everything. No one could get near me, and I could not allow myself near anyone. Everything was happening on the outside as it were, while on the inside there were just the remains of my personal holocaust.

Ten weeks after my exoneration in the Bronx Supreme Court, my brother Sean drowned accidentally. He was my closest sibling chronologically. I as priest led the town and family in mourning, but I was not there . . . so much so that it was Sean I saw and emotionally experienced when I had to say goodbye to a former friend and lover in May 1992. There was little left inside of me and I trusted no one. Yet as the moss, weeds, and grass grew over my castle ruins, I was ever so slowly beginning to be able to make my wind sheet shelter a bit sturdier.

As was stated in my defence, I was one of the few adult men in John Schaefer's life who did not abuse him. He amongst hundreds of others during my time as Campus Minister at Mount Saint Michael's Academy received the best of my pastoral care. I had an especial interest and concern for him as I knew of his history of being sexually abused and his homosexuality. He sought me out in the confessional when he was only eleven years of age. When Father Bruce's witch-hunt forced my resignation from the school, John cried in the school yard as I took my leave. It was then that I invited him amongst others to come and see me when they needed to.

Consequently, when he so publicly accused me of abusing him — encouraged by the very Church I had given my life to — my heart felt like it had been ripped out of my chest and crushed into a blob of unidentifiable gore. I felt as if my own flesh and blood had accused me. I could not distinguish between my innocence and guilt. The psycho-emotional impact of love so betrayed is such that one becomes in one's deepest self the betrayer.

The sin of so falsely and savagely destroying another person's goodness is not so much the injustice of it – and that is bad enough – No! The power of such evil is that those that do it are much more pernicious than those who kill the body. They kill the spirit, and their evil enters in and takes possession amongst the ruins of their destruction. This happened to me in the name of a church and a society that could not bear the burden of its own hatred of me and my kind. Formed as we are by those who have the deepest necessity to despise us, the bitterly contemptuous uses to which we have been put is the beginning of our history, the key to our lives, and the very cornerstone of our identities. They were successful at a level in making me a part of their self-hating homophobia, and eventually between me and them there was no between. The accuser and accused become one. The criminal – as is often the experience of rape victims – and their prey are the same. This is a frighteningly violent place to be because it has been so frighteningly violated. All this is in the name of a 'good Church, family, straight society', against the evil of homosexuality, gay, AIDS.

This space in me is still a land beyond tears. It does not help at all to recognise that much of one's trouble is produced by the really unreadable and unpredictable convolutions of one's own character. I have sat helpless and terrified before my own character, watching it spread danger and wander all over my landscape . . . and not only my own . . . It is a terrible feeling. One learns at such moments not merely how little we know, but how little whatever we know is able to help us. When Father Bruce in his madness descended on Mount St Michael's to vilify me because of his brother's death from AIDS, it was all over. I did not realise this at the time.

Through his slander he forced my resignation and eventually with the help of church and state succeeded in bringing me to court. This was not only a desecration and sacrilege of one of the most important and loving relationships of my life, but also a collapse of my inner self and a loss of strength to fight back during the court hearings. I would have succumbed to the evil surrounding me had it not been for the able defence mounted by my attorneys and the loyalty of my friends. The fact that I was innocent of the charges and found such by the court was irrelevant psycho-spiritually. In my heart of hearts the damage was done. The destruction was complete.

Every self-hating homophobic fear became me. The fact that Father Bruce's family and bishop seemed powerless over his brutal assassination on me compounded the darkness. It is noteworthy that John Schaefer's family stood by him. Up and until very recently, almost everything and everyone in church and state militated against having even the most basic human respect for homosexual people. Our lives, our loves, and even our deaths were rarely taken seriously. One need only call to mind the names, the jokes, and snide remarks so many people take as normal when talking about us. Water and blood would never again be so easily distinct for me.

How can you know what it is like to stand accused and presumed guilty amongst some of the most notorious murderers, drug barons, and rapists in the Bronx, New York? The day I was arrested, arraigned, and held amongst these people was the day that the light went out in me. The international press and media had a field day and gave me scant hope of ever ascending from this hell. As I entered the court to appear before Judge Burton Roberts, accompanied by an armed detective and two FBI agents, my knees did not want to hold me as I swallowed tears of bitter sorrow. From something that had started so innocently – belief in the Gospel human rights of sexual minorities—now I was facing trial for one of the most heinous crimes on the books!

The betrayal by the Church that I had served in New York for over twelve years made me wish I never had been born. I belonged to the wolves that would not be satiated until both I and my accuser was torn apart limb from limb. When the final verdict came down on 21 April 1989 there was nothing left inside of me but a vast emptiness of endless darkness. Yes, my innocence was proven and proclaimed by Judge Roberts, but no verdict, no about-face turn on the part of the media, could force the devil that they had poured into me to be God.

Since that soul murder, I have been uncontrollably angry at the most inappropriate times and sometimes toward people who deserved much better. I am sorry for that and thankfully such anger is on the wane. Passion is not friendly. It is arrogant, superbly contemptuous of all that is not itself, and as the very definition of passion implies the impulse to freedom, it has a mighty intimidating power. It contains a challenge; it contains an unspeakable hope. It contains a comment on all human beings, and the comment is not favourable. The loss of control in the blind search for oneself again does sometimes lead to aberrant behaviour. This does not justify it, but it does explain somewhat the unmitigated anger of a crucifixion that was demanded when it was not required.

I have also since the trial suffered serious memory loss of certain people, places, and events and been unable to cry even when people closest to me have died of AIDS. HIV/AIDS became the way of avoiding the deathliness of my own pain by focusing on that of others. While that did not invalidate my work, it did prolong the healing process. As is often the case, in such a state, we can sometimes give to others that which we most desperately need for ourselves. In fact, the giving and receiving become one. In that work, I often wondered if it would have been better if I too had been diagnosed with the virus and died with so many of my friends. When I met Billy—my life partner and now my husband—in 1993, I was incapable of responding to him. I do not blame myself for that. Here again to know all is to forgive all. I am indeed most grateful to him for being there. In that time he became my invincible summer.

Since then I have used my friends and therapist, my religion and sexuality, work and drink as a way of coping and anaesthetizing the pain. I still believe in God, and my faith in the Gospel justice of Christ is I consider the very ground of my being. As a gay man and priest, I find it almost impossible to believe in the goodness of organised religion and only most recently have begun to trust again.

What hurt most was not knowing how hurt I was. I was so unsure of my own reality that I had to continually question what it is, and then fumble with great effort onto some kind of firm ground. Having half-reached it, I hoped against hope that I would not drown again this time.

This and so much more speaks volumes of a brokenness of spirit that left me incapable at times of distinguishing between my friends and enemies, between those who hurt and tried to destroy me, and those who in their courage and their conscience stood by me. I so wanted to forgive, but for me that first meant accepting the evil of the destruction wrought in me. As John Lennon would have it, 'know your own pain'. I am still doing that at a level and it is not a pretty sight.

I often feel like a person lost between two worlds, one dead and the other not yet strong enough to be born. All the publicity after the trial did succeed in bringing attention to the injustices we all suffer under the present hegemony of power. But such attention again prevented me from looking at and attending to the woundedness that such power dialectics had wrought in me. I believe that, like 'doubting Thomas', it is only by putting my hands into the wounds can I in fact rise above them.

Saintliness means making good use of pain. There are places in the heart which do not yet exist. Suffering enters in so that they can come to be. Maybe as a result of all of this some kind of inner freedom is being brought to life in me. For freedom, not happiness as I have always said is the precious stone. One cannot cling to happiness. Happiness will submit to no clinging. Although ever so young and fragile, and consequently most vulnerable, maybe this is the apotheosis of it all? I know in a certain sense that I shall never heal from the life that I've come through, for I am healing from all of my life, not simply any one event. Yet I hope that I can learn to accept my woundedness that I can learn to live with it . . . and still find joy in being alive. The vulnerability of a tortured humanity converted into love is the miracle for which I pray.

Many of my friends after viewing the documentary *Priest on Trial* said to me, "We had no idea what you had been through!" "No you don't," I responded, "but thank you for saying that." I, too, did not know at the time 'what I had been through'. Now is the time.

I do not subscribe to the superstition that one's understanding of an event alters the event. No, the event does the altering, and the question one faces is how to live with time's brutal alteration. People invent gods, saints, and martyrs a lot of the time to prevent them from drinking what they are offered to drink from their own cup. To come up from that place where one thought one was dead means that one becomes greedy for life. And life is many things, but it is above all the touch of another. The touch of another, yes, no matter how transient, at no matter what price.

Journal Entry Number 13

Father Mychal Judge was a personal friend of mine. He was 'victim zero' at Ground Zero on September 11, 2001, made famous by that sorrowful picture flashed around the world of his dead body being carried from the flaming towers of the World Trade Center by fellow firemen on the day that has in so many ways defined the world we now live in. He was a Fire Chaplain in the City of New York. One of the last times I saw him he took me for a ride over the Brooklyn Bridge in his 'fire truck' to show me the view of the city he loved and for which he would be asked to give his life. His sudden and tragic death on 9/11 was a shock and personal loss to many of us. Three weeks after the tragedy, I travelled to New York City with my partner Billy to be present at Mychal's Month's Mind Memorial Service.

Remembering Father Mychal Judge

Mychal Judge was no gay activist. He never celebrated Mass for Dignity and to my knowledge did not ever become a formal member of any of its chapters. Yet it was at Dignity that Mychal and I first met. He had become aware through the New York media of the ongoing debacle between Cardinal O'Connor and Dignity/New York over our presence at St. Francis Xavier Church in Greenwich Village. After the issuing of the 1986 letter on *The Pastoral Care of Homosexual People* by the Vatican, Dignity/New York was ordered out of St. Francis Xavier and all priests who volunteered to celebrate Mass for Dignity were threatened with suspension and the removal of their priestly faculties. In other words they would lose their jobs as priests and be without pay or pension. This is a serious matter indeed as most priests are trained and qualified only to be priests.

Until now, the board of Dignity had only allowed priests in

good canonical standing to celebrate Mass for their membership. This was seen as some kind of tacit approval by the institutional Church for our existence as gay and Catholic. We were at this time also in the very depths of the plague. HIV/AIDS had ravaged our membership, together with so many other gay communities in the city. There was no let up in sight.

I was able to call an emergency meeting of concerned clergy at the Lesbian and Gay Community Center in Greenwich Village to respond to the crisis caused by our expulsion. Many clergy and religious attended. There were those active with our chapter and those sympathetic to the horror unfolding before us. Mychal was amongst such sympathisers.

The atmosphere at the meeting was quite tense. We felt angry and frustrated with the Archdiocese for its cruel and un-Christian treatment of Dignity priests, particularly at a time when so many of our membership were suffering and dying from HIV/AIDS. As pastors many of us felt betrayed by our Church and caught in a no-win situation.

A few of us decided to take the risk and stand with the community. Mychal came up to me and said, "Bernárd, I cannot walk this path with you, but I do support you." It was there and then that he offered us rooms at his friary of Saint Francis of Assisi on 32nd Street for our Dignity AIDS Ministry programme. By his invitation we were able to continue our pastoral outreach and weekly one-day retreats for those infected and affected by HIV/AIDS. Mychal's hospitality cushioned the hostility of the Archdiocese and saved the day for us.

In April 1988, the news broke of the FBI charges against me. I was taking refuge from the media circus inside a fellow priest's house, Father Laurence Wrenne, in Cork. Laurence, whom I hardly knew at the time and at great personal risk, gave me the hospitality of his heart and home. While there I received a phone call that Father Mychal Judge was on his way from New York to Cork. According to the message Mychal was to fill in those who wished to know 'exactly why the Archdiocese of New York had colluded with the F.B.I. to bring these charges against me'. As the New York City fire chaplain, Mychal 'had the ear of the Cardinal'. His privileged position made him privy to information that was not available to most priests.

Although I was quite suicidal at the time, the sight of Father Mychal Judge entering my room was like manna from heaven. He put his arms around me and held me for what seemed like an eternity. He did not say much. He knew what was going on and had first-hand evidence of the diocese's complicity in the false allegations made against me. He told me that I was to be made an example for all clergy who would dare to challenge the Church's teaching with regard to the lesbian, gay, and transgendered communities. He then said with that wry smile of his, "Bernárd, remember Jesus . . ."

After assuring me that he would stand with me to fight the charges, he asked could he go and visit my father, who lived about eighty miles away. My father to this day fills up with emotion when we recall this most pastoral of pastoral visits by the 'fire-fighting Franciscan from New York'. Mychal was a lonely voice of love and justice to my family in Ennis. They then thought that they could never raise their head with pride again. Mychal was a rare angel of mercy. He was central to the defence of my innocence at that crucial time.

On my return to stand trial in June 1988, Mychal met me several times to encourage and support and pray for 'our victory'. Together with many of my supporters he came to the Bronx Supreme court week in and week out to listen to the proceedings and allow due process to take its long and winding course.

Exactly one year from the time of the indictment, on 21 April 1989, the Judge declared me not only not guilty, but also innocent of all charges brought against me. None other was more jubilant than Mychal Judge. His words, "Remember Jesus, his death followed by triumph," rang out across the hallways of the court house.

Mychal and I remained in contact with each other when I moved to London in 1992. In the fall of that year he presided as chief celebrant at the funeral Mass of my cousin Eileen O'Neill Androvette and invited me to concelebrate. This he took upon himself even though the chancery of the Archdiocese had me blackballed and would not allow me to celebrate Mass anywhere in New York. Again, when I went to New York in fall 1996 to celebrate the twenty-fifth anniversary of my Ordination to priesthood, he hosted all of my priest friends at the St Francis of Assisi friary. He told them, 'not to tell the Cardinal' in his usual dry humorous way.

In seriousness or in jest, Mychal Judge saw friendship as the face of God. He was to my mind, first and foremost, a priest, and his friendship, more than any other part of this very human man, was the sacrament of his priesthood available to all. He was uniquely attuned to the depths of worth that lay hidden in each person's life.

A Touch of Spring Again

The most momentous and significant event in my life to date is that for almost fourteen years, I have been a happily married gay man. Billy and I met at a mutual friend's birthday party in March 1993. At that time, after all that had gone before and as already stated, I was in no fit state for loving. The trial, AIDS, and its aftermath had left me in shreds.

Billy from the beginning made the running. Initially I was flattered that someone so young, vibrant, and extraordinarily personable would find someone like me attractive. I passed it off and never really took his attentions seriously. What I did not realise was that Billy was, indeed serious, and deeply hurt that I would not give our relationship a chance. For almost four years I played this game. Eventually the penny dropped. He proposed to me in the beautiful and romantic city of Prague, and we had our relationship solemnly blessed and affirmed by a Cistercian priest friend on 12 September 1998.

Father Dan flew to London from the United States to be with us. This was the fiftieth anniversary of Dan's entry into the Cistercian Order. Having spent most of his life behind monastic walls and in silence, his presence was an extraordinary gift of friendship and love. Introducing himself at the beginning of the Service of Blessing as a gay Trappist monk, he instantly won the hearts of our families and many friends present to witness this precious occasion.

New beginnings like endings make us anxious and somewhat fearful. The reason is, of course, we do not 'begin ourselves.' We are 'begun' by our parents. In the ordinary course of events, neither do we 'end' ourselves. Our death and our birth – the two most important events of our lives – are beyond our control and in someone else's hands. Maybe that is why we are all so basically insecure and spend so much of our lives trying to be in control of everything. Love also, like birth and death, is beyond our control. It is a gift!

Sadly, people can't invent their mooring posts, their lovers, or their friends, anymore than they can their parents. Life gives us these, and it also takes them away. The great difficulty as I have said again and again is to say yes to life as it unfolds before us. To know love, even for a moment, is to know life. Life is God, and a life without love is a life without God . . .

As I understand it, no Holy Communion is more holy than the human communion of two people in love. If as Church we believed this, then abuse of any kind of another human being would be unthinkable. It scares me to think that we as a people are so often much more reverential around Holy Communion than 'Human Communion'. We seem to find it so much easier to adore the Christ of God's presence in the Eucharist than His presence in the body and blood of those around us. God is love, and nothing but love. This truth, of course, has nothing necessarily to do with religion. (In fact, most religious people I know relate to a God of fear rather than love.) Lovers of God, as has been said before, have no religion but God. Love alone is infallible and at the most profound level all error is the absence of love. A lot of hurt is caused in relationship by love not knowing how to love.

Whenever we attempt consciously to express love or channel it into a recognizable relationship, we are immediately restricted by the pathetic inadequacies of our physical and mental apparatus. Some believe that it is love in a relationship that grows. I don't necessarily accept that. Ordinarily one gets to know another first. Then what you get to know you choose to love or not love as the case may be. Love simply expands to contain the knowledge. Love I perceive is the skin of knowing. As we live in love with another, we get to know them more and more. Each new day is a choice, and sometimes a real challenge, to embrace that knowing of the other with love.

I have often heard it said that we stop falling in love as we grow older. I believe that we only grow older when we stop falling in love. Time is on the side of those who love. Only those who love know the meaning of time. With time, love grows younger. In fact, is there anything more beautiful than the love of two older people who have spent a lifetime struggling to make some sense of it all together? "Till the shades lengthen and evening comes. Then when the busy world is hushed and the fever of life is over," they get ready to go to God, the youngest lover there is.

I accept, although I do not always understand, that love is our ultimate environment. We are made from love and for love. To be both intensely sensual and deeply spiritual is the secret of a powerful personality. This potent blend does not produce hypocrisy, but integration and harmony, awareness and deepened sensitivity. To paraphrase Dante,

"It is love which holds the planets in orbit and blows the stars along; love which binds energy into matter, and fashions it into a myriad of different shapes and forms; love which draws the snowdrops through the frozen earth; love which scents the lilac; love which paints in hoar-frost; love which draws persons mysteriously into relationship." Love in fact is the key to our existence and to the existence of every new morning.

Julian of Norwich put it succinctly: "Love is our meaning." The creation throbs with every single gradation of loving and being in love, from the love of parents for their children and children for their parents; to the love of lovers and the love of friends and comrades. No rigid distinctions can be drawn or circled. For while love alone is the absolute, how to be loving now, is never pre-ordained beforehand. Each new situation demands a unique response and a 'new way' of loving.

In our creation and in our relationships, in our work and in our worship, love is our meaning. Again, I reiterate, we ought never to be surprised that human relationships can become confused and complicated. We are struggling within the limitations of our humanity to reflect the Divine Love from which we have come and to which we shall return. We are moved by that love, which vibrates through the universe and which is the source of every attraction and every affection.

We learn to love - as every psychologist testifies – not by being told to love but by being loved. Love is ultimately unmanageable and uncontrollable. That is why it is so frightening. It is more frightening than thunder or lightening or the fiercest of Atlantic storms, more frightening than nuclear energy, more frightening than any power known to us.

Precisely because same-sex relationships cannot in themselves create new life, they are more pellucidly entered into for their own sake. Love is its own justification. While children are indeed a blessing, they can also distract and take away from the primacy of the love relationship.

Love cannot be controlled. Love cannot be compelled. It releases us from the tyranny of reason and intellect only to imprison us helplessly in a new bondage, a bittersweet, terrible, wonderful outrageous reality. One cannot be ordered to love. One cannot be forced to stop loving. Perhaps it is the unrequited love of the great literature that illustrates most dramatically the awesome, defenceless persistency of love, enduring the agony of total rejection and never wavering. Boris Pasternak's great epic Russian novel *Doctor Zhivago* comes to mind. Love is fearsome, and this power holds all things together.

As Lonergan, the existentialist philosopher says, all true religion is based on love. It is not a code of conduct. Do this and don't do that. It does not simply mean, 'behave and you will go to heaven.' It is the radical exposure to love, exposure to this power more searing than any radiation or vital energy the earth has known. It involves laying oneself open to the possibility of sheer and utter love, recognizing and accepting that love is our beginning and our end, believing that this is the famous stone 'that turneth all to gold,' accepting that love may throw your attitudes and values upside down and yielding to the very worst that love can do. Love can kill.

Journal Entry Number 14

If It Wasn't Love

The inspiration for the title of my book – If It wasn't Love - came from a song by Mark Weigle. In this song the writer, talks about what I perceive to be the love for someone dying of HIV/AIDS. In a sense it could be seen as a modern adaptation of Saint Paul's famous and most beautiful hymn on love in 1 Corinthians13. I have been privileged to witness such love with so many friends who have died. This I saw, when against all the odds men loved men; without support or approval from family, church or society. In a certain sense it could be said that their status as outcast made them incast, in their fierce resistance to all that would deny them their love. As lovers and friends sat by the bedsides of their loved ones, day and night, I saw a loyalty that was stronger than death. Yes, 'sick by nature and against God's law, perverted and sinful,' I could not believe it anymore. It was not the sexual congress that for so many now sick and dying, had long died before them . . . Everywhere, even in the shit and vomit, peoples love for each other shone through . . . These women and men had come to know already the victory of life over death. I salute them as unsung heroes whose gift of self is written in the heart of God. To them I owe so much, for my faith in a God who is Love.

Into Summer

Where am I? Who am I as a result and consequence of all that has gone before? It has been over twenty years since the trial. In all of that time, I have tried to put my life together and move on. Billy – my husband and life partner – has been and is the gift of the God of love in that struggle.

In February 1992, after my arrival in London, I worked for an organization called CARA in Notting Hill. CARA is an aphorism for Care and Resources for People Affected and Infected by HIV and AIDS. The organization was founded by an Anglican priest, the late Father David Randall in 1989. While there, I had the privilege of meeting and working with religious women and men, together with others who were devoted to Christ, and dedicated to the Gospel. At that time, no medicine or combination therapy was known to prevent people from the real possibility of dying from their HIV diagnosis. Many of the Catholic priests and religious who came to our training and workshops to learn how to work pastorally with people diagnosed with HIV or AIDS were themselves gay. CARA provided a safe, non-judgemental environment for these men and some women to be honest about their own sexualities. Time and again, I witnessed men serving in the Catholic priesthood break down in tears because they were able to say for the first time in their lives, "I am gay."

As well as my work with CARA, I had, and still have, a private practice in psychotherapy. While I believed that psychotherapy – as in my own situation – could help these men in Catholic priesthood, on the journey from self-hate to self-love, I also realised that what was needed more than any other was a support group where they could meet and share in confidence who they were and how they coped in such a hostile world. Consequently, I formed a male Catholic clergy and religious support group in November 1992.

This group for gay clergy is, I am happy to say, in existence to this present day. At the inaugural meetings we had upwards of sixty priests present from the greater London area and further afield. Some came out of sheer curiosity, others to meet a sex date or potential boyfriend. Most were committed to their celibate vocation and simply wanted the freedom and safety to talk about themselves. Their loneliness and isolation in such a homophobic institution as Catholic priesthood was perennially on the agenda.

These good men questioned their allegiance to a Church that labelled them disordered in their nature and evil in their love. "Why," they often asked, "should I do the work of an institution that does not respect me?" Some left or were in the process of leaving. Others stayed, because their love for the Church was stronger than the hatred visited upon them or, quite simply, they had nowhere else to go. They were unskilled in anything other than priesthood.

When I initially came out of the closet in the mid-1980s, I hoped and prayed for my fellow gay priests to have the freedom to be who God created us to be. I soon realised that this was not going to happen. The situation went from bad to worse under Cardinal Ratzinger – Pope Benedict XVI - as Prefect of the Congregation of the Doctrine of the Faith. His infamous letter *On the Pastoral Care of Homosexual People* in 1986 reached a new low. This letter, for the first time in papal history denigrated ten percent of the world's population as inferior human beings.

Under his pontificate, matters would get worse before they would get better. Men who are gay were barred from seminaries. Any seminarian or priest who accepted his gay sexual orientation and tried to integrate it spiritually and psychologically into his personality was considered unacceptable for priesthood. On the other hand, those who hated, rejected, and split their orientation from the rest of their personality would be admitted. (The jargon used in the official Vatican documents was the Freudian termi-nology 'egodystonic' versus 'egosyntonic behaviour.')

What this teaching did to men in our support group who had

given a lifetime of service to the Church was devastating. The fact that so many responses from the Vatican to the child sexual abuse crisis collapsed homosexuality into paedophilia was, of course, further abuse of gay people, not to mention the continued abuse of the victims themselves. The institutional Church still will not face the fact that the endemic and systemic sexual abuse of children is caused by its own power dialectics. Any institution that legislates 'that all sex outside of marriage in the missionary position as wrong' is psychosexually sick and promotes that sickness in its teachings.

When in 1972 I first marched for civil rights for Catholics in Newry, County Down, there were hundreds – maybe thousands of Catholic priests and religious - marching with us. When in1977 I marched for civil rights in New York for the lesbian, gay, bisexual, and transgendered community, there were eight priests in Roman collars or religious garb marching. In London in 1992, there were none, Catholic or Anglican.

My priestly ministry, although still very much part of who I am, has been increasingly placed on the margins. The move by the Catholic LGBT community from Saint Anne's Anglican Church in Soho to Our Lady and Saint Gregory Church in Warrick Street in 2007 was the death knell of my public ministry to Catholic LGBT people. As one priest put it in negotiations with the Archdiocese of Westminster, "Bernárd Lynch cannot expect to celebrate Mass for the community if he is honest and open about his gayness". This priest is a 'friend' of mine, gay and sexually active himself.

Honesty by Catholic priests about their gayness is punished by job dismissal. Secrecy lies and deceit are rewarded. The thing that sours all relationship is secrecy. Secrecy eats at the soul. Some people are surprised that religion is so corruptible. They should not be. When secrecy is used to protect a 'higher order of knowledge,' it can make the keepers of the secret think of themselves as a higher order of human beings. 'Corruptio optima pessima,' goes the old saying. Blight at the top is the deepest blight. Most of the hierarchy of the Church, as I understand them psychologically, are more concerned about the submission of men to men than honesty, integrity, and openness. (There are a few exceptions, such as Bishop Willie Walsh, the retired Bishop of Killaloe, in Ireland.)

Freudian writers associate this kind of obedience with the servile rites of a boy's puberty. It encapsulates and projects this adolescent stage of development. The system of pleasure constructed in older, sometimes closeted gay men, soliciting the submission of younger closeted gay men to their will and intellect. Verbal abuse is key in this emotional submission. The pleasure of shame and humiliation is the - classical master slave - and slave master relationship. Gay men can submit to the Church and find shame in many forms. Repeated failure to be celibate, despite efforts and prayers, is a masochists, sadists, dream (or nightmare?). It has little if anything to do with the Gospel of Jesus Christ.

In my training for priesthood in the 1960s, service—not power—was what was of the ultimate concern to those in charge of our formation. We were being trained to work with the 'poorest of the poor' in the Third World and elsewhere. In that great time of renewal after Vatican II, the Gospel of social justice and human rights was the bread and butter we were fed by those who had charge over us at the African Missions Seminary in Newry, County Down, Northern Ireland. We were not trained to become lords or princes of the Church. We were in fact sent, as my Ordination card put it so succinctly, 'to bring good news to the poor and free the oppressed'. This priesthood, I continue to exercise in solidarity with all those who work for justice, when and where I am invited to celebrate Mass and the sacraments and stand shoulder to shoulder with my sisters and brothers in their struggle for equal rights. However unconscious some of us were at the beginning of the struggle of our own sexual oppression, maybe our own oppression, was the seed that impelled and the gift wrapped in thorns, that empowered us to pursue freedom, not only for ourselves but also for all people who desire to live and love in the eternal freedom of our Lover God. A God who does not know, how not to love us . . .

Journal Entry Number 15

I LIVE

I live for a Church that is on the road, walking, travelling,

Not a Church that came to a halt, or is turning in circles,

A Church that is ready to travel on the road of human history,

Together with people, sharing their history, joys and sufferings;

Not a Church that is cast down by the weight of twenty one centuries,

But a Church of the present, which not only has a history but makes history,

A Church that accompanies people on the road, ready to ask questions, to learn, to listen,

Ready to be questioned, to discuss, to search;

Not a Church that is scared or afraid of what happens in people's lives,

But a Church that sees in every challenge a new possibility for creative service,

A Church that takes time to be with people, in which people may exchange their views and experiences, in which uncertainties may be voiced,

A Church in which all people may feel at home because they feel it is theirs, a Church where questions may remain unanswered,

A Church that does not dodge the issues, that does not impose the answers,

A Church strengthened by faith in the unconditional love of God,

A Church whose love for God and people is greater than its fear and little faith,

A Church that travels even "until the night falls," that accompanies people even when it gets dark;

Not a Church that takes its leave when people do not fit in to its presupposed ideas of what is natural and what is not.

Notwithstanding the night, then people will take up their
   responsibility,
Starting with what they know from experience and building with
   what has been given them,
The gratuitous gift of a God who is Love, in whose image we are
   all co-equally made.

Finis

Circle Books

Circle is a symbol of infinity and unity. It's part of a growing list of imprints, including o-books.net and zero-books.net.

Circle Books aims to publish books in Christian spirituality that are fresh, accessible, and stimulating.

Our books are available in all good English language bookstores worldwide. If you can't find the book on the shelves, then ask your bookstore to order it for you, quoting the ISBN and title. Or, you can order online—all major online retail sites carry our titles.

To see our list of titles, please view www.Circle-Books.com, growing by 80 titles per year.

Authors can learn more about our proposal process by going to our website and clicking on Your Company > Submissions.

We define Christian spirituality as the relationship between the self and its sense of the transcendent or sacred, which issues in literary and artistic expression, community, social activism, and practices. A wide range of disciplines within the field of religious studies can be called upon, including history, narrative studies, philosophy, theology, sociology, and psychology. Interfaith in approach, Circle Books fosters creative dialogue with non-Christian traditions.

And tune into MySpiritRadio.com for our book review radio show, hosted by June-Elleni Laine, where you can listen to authors discussing their books.

MySpiritRadio